A Sorrow Shared

A Combined Edition of the Nouwen Classics
In Memoriam and *A Letter of Consolation*

D1113866

HENRI J.M. NOUWEN

foreword by Barbara Brown Taylor

AVE MARIA PRESS **AVE** Notre Dame, Indiana

A Sorrow Shared first published in 2010 by Ave Maria Press, Inc.

A Letter of Consolation © 1982 by Henri J.M. Nouwen. Published by arrangement with HarperOne, an imprint of HarperCollins Publishers.

In Memoriam © 1980, 2005 by Ave Maria Press, Inc.

Foreword © 2010 by Barbara Brown Taylor.

www.avemariapress.com

Founded in 1865, Ave Maria Press is a ministry of the United States Province of Holy Cross.

ISBN-10 1-59471-253-0   ISBN-13 978-1-59471-253-1

Cover design by Dave Scholtes.

Text design by John Robert Carson.

Printed and bound in the United States of America.

Library of Congress Cataloging-in-Publication Data is available.

Contents

Foreword

$\mathcal{W}$hen I arrived at Yale Divinity School in the fall of 1973, Henri Nouwen was not yet Henri Nouwen—or at least not yet the bestselling author of dozens of books, whose reflections on prayer, ministry, suffering, and compassion would become lifelines for hundreds of thousands of readers worldwide.

In 1973 he was still a lecturer in pastoral theology whose new book, *The Wounded Healer*, had come out the year before. He lived in Porter Hall, the men's dormitory, where he famously left his door unlocked for anyone in need of counsel or company. Since memory fails, I cannot tell you whether he continued to do so after someone stole all of his stereo equipment, but the invitation remained open: Henri was there for anyone who needed him, day or night.

Students who watched television in the student lounge would sometimes look up to see him coming through the door with a stack of books pinned under his chin. This meant that Henri had published a new title, and that his box of complimentary author's copies had just arrived. Staggering from couch to chair, he would pull one off the top of the stack for each of us, then disappear back into his apartment with the leftovers. In this way I acquired *Out of Solitude* (1974) and *Reaching Out* (1975)—not because I was special to Henri but simply, I think, because he had no one else to give them to.

I became his student, which gave me opportunity to learn what a complicated person he was—a celibate who taught courses in human sexuality, a solitary who wrote volumes about intimacy, a solemn man who loved circus clowns. He spent six months at the Abbey of the Genesee in upstate New York during my middle year, returning with a new book manuscript in hand (*The Genesee Diary*).

When I read it, I was struck once again by the distance between Henri-in-person and Henri-on-the-page. In person, he sometimes shook with the effort of containing his rage at those who had disappointed him. On the page, he pulled his heart open with both of his hands so that anyone who wanted could walk in. Henri's very great gift, both in person and on the page, was to struggle publicly with the essential business of becoming human before God.

Never was this truer than when he wrote of his mother's death. Maria Nouwen died precipitously in 1978, two years after my graduation from Yale. By then my only contact with her son was through his books, so that I did not learn how this seminal event had affected him until I read *In Memoriam* in 1980, followed by *A*

Letter of Consolation in 1982. While neither volume is bigger than a slice of bread, both are full of Nouwen's characteristic head-on honesty and Catholic faith.

In Memoriam is the shorter of the two. Nouwen wrote it, he said, because so much happened in the last, quick days of his mother's life that he feared it would escape him unless he found words to frame his experience. The words he found are deep and defenseless, showing the reader how intimately his vocation as a son nested inside his vocation as a priest. Nouwen read psalms to his mother, gave her last rites, celebrated the Eucharist at her funeral, and prayed over her grave. His priesthood offered him a way to stay present to his whole family during a time of great grief. It offered him a "safe house" in which to dwell, until he could discover the "strange joy" of becoming "a man alone in a new way."

A Letter of Consolation is a very different book. The subject is still his mother's death, but the audience this time is his father—a retired lawyer both known and feared, Nouwen says, for his irony and sarcasm, for his sharp wit and critical analysis. Feeling "strong enough to raise the question of our most basic human infirmity," Nouwen decides to write his father a long letter during the last days of Lent in 1979. While the putative purpose of the letter is to comfort his father, the deeper reason is to give in to his own grief. By putting his thoughts on paper, Nouwen hopes to unite his pain with that of his father—and it works. As he sits writing in his little room at the Abbey of the Genesee, he notices the first tears he has shed for his mother coming from his eyes.

A Letter of Consolation is rawer (and therefore truer to life) than *In Memoriam*. Early on, Nouwen speaks convincingly of how important it is to befriend death. If we could really do it, he says, then we would be free people. Nearer the end of the book, he says just as convincingly that "If anyone should protest against death it is the religious person, the person who has increasingly come to know God as the God of the living."

Yet this tension is the strength of the book, not its weakness. Like the composer of a symphony that moves from major to minor chords and back again, Nouwen plays all the keys at his disposal. When a finger slips, he does not stop. He just keeps pounding out the chords until he reaches the mystical resolution that seems to surprise even him, and may surprise you too. That this moment comes on a brilliant Easter after a stormy Good Friday will seem very fitting to anyone familiar with Nouwen's work. Once again, his life in Christ turns out to be the key that opens his life to everything and everyone else.

While these books go together, they do not equal a handbook on grief. Instead, they testify to the truth that every death lays bare what really matters, and what really matters will not be the same for any two readers. "In many different ways," Nouwen says, his mother told him and still tells him "that what is most universal is also most personal."

Since I first read both of these books while my own parents were still alive, I read them as messages in bottles, sent from an island I knew I would one day visit but that I hoped to stay away from as long as possible. Thirty years later I am sitting on the beach with both messages in my lap. The good news is that they are true, which means that they are also deeply consoling—even for those whose love is not this pure, whose faith is not this real—for Nouwen is right that we find comfort where our wounds hurt most, and he has never been afraid to meet us there.

BARBARA BROWN TAYLOR
Easter 2010

In Memoriam

Introduction

My mother died on Monday, October 9, 1978, at 6:14 p.m. It was one of the few moments when I was not at her bedside. I had just left the hospital room to make a telephone call. When I reentered the room, my brother looked at me and said, "She is dead." My father had put his head on the bed and was crying softly. My sister and younger brother, who had been standing outside the room talking, came in and looked at her silent face. It was over now.

The doctor came in, listened to her heart and said, "Yes, she has died." Then we prayed. I struggled to find the words which were our words: words of grief, words of gratitude, words of hope. It was a very intimate moment. My mother lay there, still and in peace. Looking at her, we prayed, "Lord, lead her now to your house and give us the courage to continue our lives, grateful for all she has given to us." Then we left the room where we had spent the last five days, hour by hour witnessing her pain and struggle. We knew that she would never be with us again.

I want to write about these last days with my mother. So much happened in those days that I fear it will escape me in the whirlwind of everyday life unless I can find words to frame my experience. I want to express how during those days her love, her care, her faith, and her courage became more visible to me than ever before, and how I came to know in a new way what it meant to be her son. But it is so difficult and painful. Every word seems to be the wrong word, every expression seems to do violence to what I feel, every page of praise or gratitude seems to distort that gently built network of love that was her life. Yet, not writing is worse; not writing is like not mourning, not feeling the pain, not tasting the bitterness of her farewell.

I know that it would be possible to continue, telling myself that she died as we all have to die; to be brave, strong, self-composed and firm. I know how to answer the condolences of friends who say, "I am sorry to hear that your mother died." I have my sentences ready: not so many as to bore them, not so few as to appear abrupt or cool. By now, I have used them many times: "Thank you . . . yes . . . it all happened faster than we thought . . . she and my father came to visit me in the United States . . . when she arrived at Kennedy Airport she felt very tired and could not eat . . . the doctor, a friend, found jaundice caused by a tumor . . . she returned with my father after only four days . . . in Holland she underwent surgery . . . the cancer proved widespread . . . she regained consciousness following the operation but died six days later from a complication in her lungs. . . ."

I have no idea how often I have uttered these insignificant phrases. Why do I repeat these empty sentences? They explain nothing. Worse, they seem to hide more than they reveal. Every time I use these words I keep wondering why I am so unable to communicate the mystery of which I have become a part, the new vision that has disclosed itself to me. The endless dialogue, "I am sorry" . . . "Yes, I am sad," often touches off a strange weariness instead of bringing comfort. Even so, I am deeply grateful to everyone who expresses sorrow and am quite eager to share my grief with anyone. But something is taking place that is too important to be confined to the few phrases that I have already used so often. I must try at least to say more.

My mother died. This event cannot claim any uniqueness. It is among the most common of human experiences. There are few sons and daughters who have not experienced or will not experience the death of their mother, suddenly or slowly, far away or close by. Still, I want to reflect on this event because, although it is not unusual, exceptional, or extraordinary, it remains in many ways unknown and unfathomed. It is indeed in the usual, normal, and ordinary events that we touch the mystery of human life. When a child is born, a man and woman embrace, or a mother or father dies, the mystery of life reveals itself to us. It is precisely in the moments when we are most human, most in touch with what binds us together, that we discover the hidden depths of life. This is the reason why I feel free now to speak about my mother, whom I have loved so dearly and whose death is causing me such deep grief. In many different ways she has told me, and still tells me, that what is most universal is also most personal.

I remember how embarrassing it always was for my mother when I would praise her in the presence of others. She did not like me to speak about her. But now she no longer holds me back; she can no longer be embarrassed. Now she is no longer just my mother; she is a woman whose son wants to speak about what she has revealed to him, not only in her life but also in her death. In life she belonged to a few, in death she is for all.

1

*I*t all happened so fast—and slow! As I flew from New York to Amsterdam, I realized that I was going to say farewell to my mother. As often as I had made that same trip, this time it seemed unreal. Already I felt my perceptions changing as my immediate surroundings seemed to fade away. I had a hard time listening to the pleasant lady on my right who told me about her daughter's college. I could not bring myself to buy earphones to listen to music or to follow the sound of the movie. I could not make myself read a book that would draw me into the complexities of other people's lives. Above the cold North Atlantic, I felt alone. Not lonely, not depressed, not anxious, not afraid, but alone in a new way. My mother was dying. She was waiting for me to come, she wanted to see me and to pray with me. It was this reality that began to fill my mind as the plane carried me home. I realized that something very new was happening to me.

Just a month ago I had been flying from Jerusalem to Rome. A sixty-year-old man sitting next to me explained that he was returning to the United States to attend the funeral of his brother. I remember feeling uncomfortable, somewhat embarrassed, and self-conscious. I even felt some irritation because I had to sit for three hours beside this man with whom I could not have a "normal" conversation. Now I was the one who might embarrass or irritate my fellow human beings, people who did not want to be pulled out of their joyful anticipation of a happy holiday. I realized that sorrow is an unwelcome companion and that anyone who willingly enters into the pain of a stranger is truly a remarkable person.

At seven o'clock in the morning I finally walked through the long hallways of Schiphol airport. Two hours later I entered the hospital room in Nijmegen where my mother lay in pain. From the moment I saw her I knew that something totally new was beginning. I smiled and she looked at me, grateful that I had come. I kissed her forehead and touched her hand. Words were hardly possible or necessary. The only thing that seemed important was that we were together.

She was looking at me with the same eyes with which she had so often looked at me—when I went to the seminary, when I became a priest, when I left to live in the States: eyes expressing a love that could never be separated from pain. Maybe that was what had always touched me most deeply—her eyes, in which love and sadness were never completely separated. How often had I seen tears in her eyes when I left again after a day, a week, or a month at home! How often had I looked into that lovely face, which expressed so beautifully that love causes pain!

I can still see her waving from the quay of Rotterdam Harbor as the large ship *Statendam* slowly left its berth, taking me on my first trip to the United States. I can still see her waving as I passed the "passengers only" sign and walked through the airport gates. I can still see her waving from the door of the house as I was driven away in my brother's car. And—the clearest memory of all because it happened hundreds of times—I see her waving from the platform as the train rolled away from the station, making her figure smaller and smaller and smaller.

Always there was a smile and a tear, joy and sadness. From the moment of my birth when her tears merged with smiles, it has always been that way.

Now there was no doubt that she was dying; it was so clearly written on her face. I knew that we both knew. But there were no words. I bent over her face. So close, so intimate, so gentle, so painful. The tears in her eyes made me realize that while she was glad that I had come, she was also sad that we could now do no more than just look at each other—and pray.

"Shall I pray?" I asked softly. She seemed pleased and nodded. Knowing she would have asked me this if she had possessed the strength to speak, I realized that the words of the psalms would make it possible to communicate with each other in new ways. For a year now we have prayed with the same prayerbook. During the many evenings we spent together we had read the hymns and psalms of the evening prayer, finding in them a time of shared tranquility. When I opened the book it was all so very normal, familiar, and safe.

> Like the deer that yearns
> for running streams,
> so my soul is yearning
> for you, my God.
>
> My soul is thirsting for God,
> the God of my life;
> when can I enter and see
> the face of God?
>
> My tears have become my bread,
> by night, by day,
> as I hear it said all the day long:
> "Where is your God?"
>
> These things will I remember
> as I pour out my soul:
> how I would lead the rejoicing crowd
> into the house of God . . .
>
> Why are you cast down, my soul,
> why groan within me?
> Hope in God; I will praise yet again,
> my savior and my God.
>
> —PSALM 41

As these words were slowly shaped by my lips, covering her like a gentle cloud, I knew that we were closer than ever. Although she was too ill to smile, too weak to say thanks, too tired to respond, her eyes expressed the joy we felt in simply being together. The psalms had a power which I had not recognized before. They lifted the veil of sentimentality. As soon as the words of the psalms were spoken, there was a strength, a power, and a divine realism between us. There was a joyful clarity. A mother was dying, her son was praying, God was present and all was good.

As she looked into my eyes, I knew that my gratitude for her presence in my life would live on within me. As I looked into her eyes, I knew that she would die grateful for her husband, her children and grandchildren, and the joyful life that had always surrounded her. "Why are you cast down, my soul, why groan within me? Hope in God; I will praise yet again, my savior and my God." There was a surge of energy that did not come from an ailing woman or a heartbroken man. There was a sense of truth that embraced us both. I did not cry or feel the desire to do so. She did not cry or try to say a word. We were together in a moment of truth, a moment that we wanted to taste together.

How long would it last? How many hours, days, or months would we be able to have together? "Why worry about it?" I thought. "Why not simply be here to taste and see the goodness of the Lord at this very moment?"

Then I kissed her again and said, "I am going to get a few hours' sleep. I need it after the long plane trip. I will see you tonight." I pressed a sign of the cross on her forehead with my thumb and added, "Good-bye . . . sleep well." Then, after quietly leaving her room, I went to the house where my father and sister were waiting for me. I felt very peaceful, very strong, very joyful. We were together, and we were surrounded by strength.

2

$\mathcal{W}$hen I returned in the evening her eyes had changed. I looked at her but she could no longer respond with her eyes. I pressed her hand but she could no longer hold mine. My brother and sister were with me at her bedside. I said, "Mother, I want to give you the sacrament of the sick. . . . I want to give you the oil of healing, and we want to pray for you together." I bent over her and she said softly, "It is hard for me to think, you know what is good." After lighting a candle, I prayed for healing, for new life, for strength in this moment of crisis, and for the courage to surrender to God's will. It was at this moment, when I crossed her three times with the oil as she lay quietly on the bed, that I realized she had turned her eyes to God.

Until this hour she had been thinking and speaking about us, her husband, her children, her friends. Now it seemed that the time had come to face God. Her eyes had turned inward. She no longer saw her husband Laurent, and her children, Harrie, Paul and Marja, Wim and Heiltjen, Laurine and Marc. She was seeing other realities, more awesome, more frightening, more captivating, but also more decisive.

Shortly after this quiet moment—the intimate celebration with a burning candle, a few softly spoken words and the touch with oil—the struggle began. We were not prepared for it; we had never even thought about her death as a death with a struggle. We had not anticipated anxiety, fear, and agony. Why should we? Hers was a beautiful, gentle, generous life, marked by giving all there was to give. It could not possibly end in a restless, painful, torturous struggle. Peaceful people should die a peaceful death; faithful people should die a quiet death; loving people should die a gentle death. But is this true? Who am I to formulate simplistic equations and logical sequences? Since I do not even know why we live, why should I expect to know how we are to die? If life is a mystery, why should death be viewed as a reality within our grasp and understanding?

The soft oil I had given her was much more than oil that points to healing. The apostle James certainly had healing uppermost in his mind when he wrote: "Any one of you who is ill should send for the elders of the church, and they must anoint the sick person with oil in the name of the Lord and pray over him. The prayer of faith will save the sick person and the Lord will raise him up again; and if he has committed any sins, he will be forgiven" (Jas 5:14–15). But oil is not only a symbol of healing. It is also a symbol of struggle. Ancient warriors anointed their bodies before battle, and modern-day wrestlers use oil to limber their muscles and make their bodies agile.

Could it be that I had applied oil on my own mother to help prepare her for the final battle? Is it not possible that she who lived her life in such close union with God had also come to know the power of the Evil One more intimately than many others? Is it inconceivable that she who had spent so many hours in prayer was also most aware of the one whom we call "the Tempter"? Is it not possible that great faith reveals the possibility of doubt, that great love reveals the possibility of hate, that great hope reveals the possibility of despair?

I began to realize that the oil I had given her was a sign that a great battle needed to be fought. Indeed, it is the ultimate battle, the magnitude of which is understood by only a very few.

This is more than a pious attempt to explain a difficult death. Mother had told me not just once, but often, that she was afraid to die. Many people will say the same, but mother meant something very concrete, very specific, very unambiguous. Three weeks before her death she said to me, "I am afraid to die, not to go to the hospital, not to undergo surgery, not to suffer pain. I am afraid to appear before God and show him my life." It was this great encounter that frightened her. She was so deeply impressed by God's awesome greatness and had become so aware of her own nothingness that the great encounter could only frighten her.

Maybe *fear* was not the best word; perhaps she meant *dread*, the overpowering knowledge of the great abyss between God and his creatures. That awesome awareness meant a momentous struggle, a battle, a fight. How can a human being face God and live? What is there to hold on to except faith, hope, and love? Everything else seems to vanish in this terrifying hour—even husband, children, grandchildren, and a beautifully lived life with its joys and pains. At the moment of death only God matters. The struggle is a lonely one. Indeed, the oil is a profound symbol at the hour of death.

Shortly after I had given the sacrament of the sick to my mother, she entered into a long, drawn-out agony. My brother, who had decided to stay with her a little longer while my sister and I went home, saw that the quiet peacefulness had left her and that a restlessness had started to take over. Not only did mother's eyes no longer seem to focus on those around her, but her movements no longer had a specific direction and her whole body appeared to be gripped by fear. When my brother told me what was happening, we decided that from then on we wanted to be with her every moment of the day and night. We followed her agony from minute to minute, from hour to hour, from day to day.

How great is the mystery of our life! Not one of us had suspected that we would be witnessing this painful struggle of the woman we loved so much. There was nothing we could do except be there, hold her arms, which moved restlessly in the air, gently wipe her perspiring forehead, and carefully fluff up the pillows, offering every little bit of comfort we could.

I still wonder what I was feeling during those hours. I felt powerless, small, and helpless, but also peaceful, strong, and quiet. I was seeing and feeling something I had never seen or felt before, an experience that to be described would require words that have not yet been found: powerless yet strong, sad yet peaceful, broken yet whole. I still do not fully understand this new emotion. One thing, however, I can articulate because I felt it so clearly: I was blessed to be part of a moment of truth.

Everything was truthful, there was no lie. Mother was dying and nobody denied it. Although her suffering was deep and mysterious, it was not hidden from us. We experienced the privilege of being close to her suffering, intimately connected with her pain, deeply united with her agony. Looking at mother's blank eyes, guiding her restless arms in their haphazard movements, and repeating words of consolation and comfort, I was not afraid, I was not anxious, not nervous, not self-conscious. I have never felt so strongly that the truth can make us free. It was a very sacred moment, and I was blessed to be there.

The world outside—the cars on the streets, the voices in the hospital corridors, the students in the United States, the lectures to give, the conferences to attend, the articles to write and the books to discuss—suddenly appeared illusory and permeated by shadows of untruth. The truth was here, now, in this room:

mother was dying, in mortal struggle with the great powers of life and death.

She no longer saw me or my father, my brothers, or my sister, but she saw what we could not see. From the depths of her struggle she cried out to God, "O God, my God, my Father, my God." These words—words she had said thousands of times during her life—now came from the center of her being and formed a long, agonizing cry.

As the long hours passed into longer nights and days, her cry became deeper and stronger. Bending over her, I heard her words of prayer: "My Father who art in heaven, I believe, I hope, I love . . . My God, my Father . . ." I knew that this was the struggle of the great encounter. I wanted to give her the freedom she needed to enter into this lonely hour, to give her the space where this most mysterious of events could take place. I knew that she needed more than comforting words; she needed whatever support we could give her in this struggle of faith. With my father, brothers, and sister, I prayed the prayers she hinted at—the Our Father, the Creed, the Hail Mary, and the Litany of the Mother of God. In this way, we felt as if we offered her the words she could no longer speak herself, surrounding her with a shield of prayer that allowed her to fight her lonely battle.

Why? Why were we witnessing such pain and agony in a woman whose life had been one of goodness, gentleness, tenderness, and love? Why did she who had been so generous and self-giving have to enter into this torturous hour? Why all this pain, this suffering, this struggle?

During the days of mother's dying, I heard that question repeated frequently. Often, friends suggested that it was unfair for this lovely woman to suffer such a painful death. Many were adamant that she did not deserve such a wrenching struggle. But do we really understand?

Slowly, as the long hours and days passed, I began to wonder if mother's struggle did not in fact reveal the awesome truth of God's love. Who was more loving than Jesus? Who suffered more than he? Jesus' life of faithful service did not end in a peaceful, tranquil death. He who was without sin suffered an agony of immeasurable depth; his cry on the cross, "My God, my God, why have you forsaken me?" still echoes down through the centuries.

Is it this agony that mother was called to share? Is it this cross that she was invited to feel more deeply than many others? I do not know. I cannot say yes or no to these questions. What really took place during the hours of her death cannot be explained or made understandable. But the thought that she who had loved so many, given so much, and felt so deeply, was called to be united with Christ even in his agony, did not leave me during these days.

Friends kept saying to me, "Your mother always thought of others first." That is true. She lived for others:

for her husband, her children, her grandchildren, her friends. She indeed had the mind of Christ, always considering the other person to be better than herself. But that does not necessarily lead to a smooth death. Why do we think that Christian death is an easy death? Why do we believe that the hope for a life with Christ will make our death like a gentle passage? A compassionate life is a life in which the suffering of others is deeply felt, and such a life may also make one's death an act of dying with others. When I saw mother's battle, her cry of hope and faith, I wondered if she was not crying with the many others for whom she had lived.

In Jesus' agony we see the agony of the world in all its gripping intensity: "He began to feel sadness and anguish. Then he said. . . 'My soul is sorrowful to the point of death'" (Mt 26:37). Is not every human being who wants to live with the mind of Christ also called to die with the mind of Christ? This can mean very different things for different people. It certainly does not have to mean the struggle mother suffered. Yet it seems at least important to understand that those who live with Christ must also be prepared to die with him, to be willing even to accept the invitation to enter into his agony.

What then is this agony? Is it fear of God, fear of punishment, fear of the immensity of the divine presence? I do not know, but if I have any sense of what I saw, it was more profound. It was the fear of the great abyss which separates God from us, a distance which can only be bridged by faith. The test comes when everything that is dear to us slips away—our home and those we love, our body and its many ways of living, our mind and its caring thoughts—and there is absolutely nothing left to hold on to. It is then that one must have the faith to surrender to a loving Lord, to believe that he will not allow us to fall into a cruel and bottomless canyon, but will bring us to the safe home which he has prepared for us. My mother knew her weaknesses and shortcomings. Her long life of deep prayer had not only revealed to her God's greatness, but also her own smallness; not only God's openheartedness, but also her own fearfulness; not only God's grace, but also her own sinfulness. It seemed that it was precisely her lifelong conversation with God that made her death such an agonizing event. At the hour of death all becomes faith. Faith in God, who knows every fiber of our being and loves us in spite of our sins, is the narrow gate which connects this world with the next.

What am I talking about? Am I making an existential drama out of the death of a woman who lived a good life but died a painful death? The doctors and nurses in the hospital, who surrounded my mother with competent care, neither could nor would speak with the words and concepts that I have been using. They referred to a growing lack of oxygen, a hard-to-explain restlessness, and a difficult-to-understand groaning. But is that all there is to say? No doubt lack of oxygen creates anxiety, but not all anxiety is experienced as a struggle of faith in the moment of the encounter with God himself. What am I saying when I speak about a sharing in Christ's agony? Some, mostly the medical staff, interpreted her struggle primarily as a physical response to a very radical operation. Others, who had known her piety, perceived it as the emergence of old memories and deeply embedded routine phrases repeated during a state of semi-consciousness. But I saw something else. I saw my own mother entering into that moment in which we are totally alone with God, in which the final decision of life must be made: the decision of faith.

3

*H*ow will things be and feel when she is no longer part of my life? Over the years I have often asked myself this question, even though I realized that there was no answer because the experience was so totally unknown. I became aware that during the years of my childhood, adolescence, and adulthood, the bonds with my mother had grown so deep and so intimate that I would never be able to know their full significance before her death. Every time I tried to think of my life without her, my mind went blank, leaving me completely unable to imagine anything. But increasingly I sensed the mysterious depth of the relationship between mother and child. I had read enough psychology books to know about possessive mothers, dependent sons, and deep, unresolved ties between children and parents. Yet I realized that all this failed to explain our relationship; there was much more to be understood.

From her I had come to feel an unqualified acceptance which had little to do with my being good or bad, successful or unsuccessful, close by or far away. In her

I had come to sense a love that was free from demands and manipulations, a love that gave me a sense of belonging that could be found nowhere else. It is hard to express exactly what I was sensing, but the word "belonging" comes closest to it. She represented a reality of goodness and safety which was much larger than herself. When, even in the midst of turmoil and restlessness, conflicts and failures, I continued to feel that life is ultimately good and benign, I knew that she had been, and still was, my teacher. It had very little to do with frequent visits, letters, or telephone calls; it had even less to do with discussing issues or making plans; and it had nothing at all to do with day-to-day decisions. With the Atlantic Ocean separating our homes, there were few occasions for the simpler forms of dependency.

When I thought to myself, "It is better to live than not to live, it is better to struggle and fail than not to struggle at all," I knew that she had something to do with it. Maybe I can say that she gave me that basic sense of the goodness of life that allowed me to move freely and fearlessly to many places, to live with many different people and in many different circumstances, and to feel free far from home.

If I had told her any of these things, she probably would have felt confused, embarrassed, or even offended. Or perhaps she would have simply called me a sentimentalist. The fact of the matter is that I could not have said any of this to her. It is only now, after she has gone, after she has been buried, that these thoughts and words do not seem silly or romantic to me. They are simply the expression of a truth.

I never did arrive at an answer to the question, "How will life be when she is no longer present on the horizon of my thoughts, feelings, and emotions?" Now I realize that I have to grow into the answer slowly, gently, carefully, and very patiently. The answer will not come in the form of a thought or an insight, but in the form of a new love.

As I looked at my father, my brothers, and my sister standing around her in the hospital, I began to realize that she would never abandon us. That deep sense of safety she had given to us, that feeling of belonging to a world which could be trusted, would not die with her but would anchor itself more deeply in our being.

I saw this first in my father. I had often worried about his sorrow and grief should mother die before him. I had often wondered about his life alone after a long and happy life with her. But when I saw him looking at his dying wife, I realized that there were hidden resources that I had not seen before. It was the strength of a love which cannot be destroyed by death. I saw power, courage, and freedom breaking through his tears. It was then that I knew that mother's death would not crush him. I also saw this same strength in my two brothers and their wives, in my sister and her husband, all of whom radiated a care, love, and concern that revealed far more than the sorrow of losing their dearly loved mother. I felt it in myself. I felt strong, yes, even strangely joyful, during these days. It was the joy of feeling a great love binding us together, a love which she had given us and which was not going to be taken away from us.

It is difficult to put into words what I want to say. Such words as "love" and "care" can so easily be interpreted in an emotional way, and yet none of us standing around mother's bed were ever very good at expressing our feelings toward one another. In fact, during these long hours of waiting, none of us said anything very new. The words were the same as always. Yet, as we watched her life slowly fade away, we all sensed that the bond between us which she had created was growing stronger and deeper.

This new closeness that we began to feel was something far greater than what is expressed by the remark, "You still have each other." We became for each other new people with new lives and new perspectives. Life started to reveal itself in new ways. I was not simply saying farewell to her; I was also letting go of something in myself that had to die. I also perceived this in my father, my brothers, and my sister. Old boundaries that had maintained certain distances between us were being lifted so that new intimacies could grow.

Only in this context is it possible for me to understand fully why it became so easy for us to pray together. As children we had prayed together before going to bed. Although we still pray together at table, it is only infrequently that we enter together into the intimacy of prayer.

But as we found ourselves gathered around mother's bed, our prayer was easy, free, spontaneous, and natural. It offered us words of greater power and meaning than any of the words we could have said to one another. It gave us a sense of unity which could not be created by speculations on the nature of mother's illness or her chances of recovery. It provided a sense of togetherness that was more given than made, and it created a place in which we could rest together.

Some of the prayers we said were ones that mother had taught us as children, prayers that now came to mind again after years of absence. Some were prayers which had never been spoken before, while others were prayers which have been repeated over the centuries by men and women in pain and agony.

The prayers we said together became the place where we could be together without fear or apprehension. They became like a safe house in which we could dwell, communicating things to each other without having to grope for inadequate, self-made expressions. The psalms, the Our Father, the Hail Mary, the Creed, the Litany of the Saints, and many other prayers formed the walls of this new house, a safe structure in which we felt free to move closer to each other and to mother, who needed our prayers in her lonely struggle.

Thus the days and nights passed—a sequence of prayer, silence, and short conversations. We had a deep sense that she experienced our presence and could perceive the gentle rhythm of our prayers. Often we would move close to her and tell her that we were there, tell her about our love and our gratitude. But mostly we just remained silent. During the first days we had read books or magazines to pass the time. Now we simply looked at her, and at each other, letting the long hours of the days and nights deepen our presence. From this time on all that mattered was simply to be with her without asking or demanding anything.

4

*A*fter three days of struggle mother was exhausted. She no longer had the energy to fling her arms about in anxious movements; she could no longer even mumble prayers or cry out to God in audible words. The doctor who had seen her long, painful struggle said, "For her it has been like running up and down a long staircase for three days. Now there is no strength left."

We sat by her bedside, watching her breathing becoming shorter and shorter every hour. For three days we had been struggling with her, holding on to her from both sides of the bed, speaking words of comfort, praying quietly or out loud. In the past week there had been moments when we thought about the possibility of survival, brief fantasies that mother might somehow come back home and once again be with us. But, above all, there was the desire to see her open her eyes, smile, and say a few words.

The hope for a single moment of recognition, or perhaps just a few words, held us all in its grip. We kept asking ourselves and each other: "Can she hear? Does she know that we are all with her? Does she feel our love and concern? Can she understand anything we are saying? Does she sense that we are praying for her?"

Sometimes there seemed to be a small sign of recognition, a glimmer of understanding. But mostly her eyes remained without expression and her hands no longer responded to our touch. Father looked at her and then said softly, "I know there are so many things you would like to say, but you cannot—it's all right, we are with you." While he was speaking these words, I felt our immense desire for a response, just a little response, a word, a nod, a smile, a movement of the hand. It seemed that we were begging for more contact.

How great is the human desire for contact! After thirty, forty, or fifty years of living together, with its innumerable conversations, discussions, and hours of intimate exchanges, we still wanted another sign. We were still hoping that maybe mother would bless us one more time. At times I felt guilty for desiring yet another gift from her who had given us so much. I even felt selfish and greedy. But the desire was there, strong and powerful, and slowly we had to accept that she had given us enough, more than enough.

As the hours passed it became clear that she was dying, that we would never again receive another word or gesture from her. Although we had known for the past three days that she was dying, now the awareness of finality began to touch us. There would be no new chances for expressions of thanks or regret, joy or sadness. There would be no opportunities to change anything. Never. Her life was coming to an end and our relationship with her was moving into the realm of memory. We realized that the way in which we had been her husband, son, or daughter was now defined forever. The question was no longer, "How are we going to interact with her?" but, "How are we going to remember her?"

As we looked at her—totally exhausted from the struggle, breathing short breaths—we found our memories beginning to summarize all that had been. My father looked at me and said very quietly, "I see my whole life with your mother passing in front of my eyes: the first time we met, our first happy days, our first little disagreements and conflicts, our hard days of working together, your birth and all that followed until now. . . . It just stands in front of my eyes like a small picture I can look at." Looking at him, I sensed the brevity of life in my bones: a flash, a moment, a breath . . . arrival and departure . . . yesterday and today . . . all compressed in one blink of an eye. There was immense tenderness in that moment, an intimacy that I had not known before. It was not a case of the wise speaking to the unwise, the old to the young, the experienced to the inexperienced. There were no longer wise and unwise, old and young, experts and untrained. Here in the presence of death, we were indeed the same, feeling our equality as a grace.

The end came very quietly. I had left the room to make a phone call while my youngest brother and my sister were walking in the hospital corridor, talking a little between the times they spent at mother's bedside. My father and younger brother sat on either side of mother's bed, following her breathing. It had become very quiet. The nurses had just rearranged the bed, washed mother's hands and face, and combed her hair. All had become very quiet.

It was six o'clock in the evening. Father looked at her with full attention, expecting that she might still live for many hours. But then he noticed a definite slowing down of her breathing, saw her neck muscle make two more movements, and realized that she had stopped breathing. Everything was still, very still. Father bent his head, kissed her hand, and cried. Then he said to my brother, "She has died; call your brothers and sister." As we stood around her bed we prayed the same prayers we had said so often during the past days. But now I added for the first time the words we would say in the long days to come: "May eternal light enlighten her that she may rest in peace."

She had simply stopped breathing. That was all. With carefully chosen words, father told us about the final seconds of her life, how the end had come with a slight quiver of her neck. "It was hardly noticeable," he said, with a soft smile in his eyes. It had been so undramatic, so quiet. It had hardly been an event. For a moment I felt sad because I had not been in the room.

But then I realized that I should be grateful that father and mother had been so close in those last moments. I recognized that it was a gift that he, and not I, could tell the story.

5

It was a foggy Saturday morning. When I opened the curtains of my bedroom and saw a thick mist hanging over the fields, I thought that for many people it might be hard to reach this small, isolated village. At eleven o'clock, mother's funeral would take place. Following the service we would bury her in the small cemetery on the site of the old church which had been destroyed in the war.

As I looked out into the mist, I tried to become fully aware of my feelings on this day. But it was difficult to come close to my own inner life. There was the sadness of the farewell, but also the gladness of welcoming the friends who were coming from many directions to join us in our prayer. This was the day to remind myself, my family, and my friends that she had indeed left us, that she would no longer make breakfast, call our names, or appear with her gentle smile in the living room. I had to let the truth that she had left us descend deeply into my heart.

My mind returned to one of the most difficult and saddest moments of the week. It occurred when I returned with my father to our home. We had spoken quietly about her during the forty-five-minute drive from the hospital to the small country town where my parents have lived for the last eight years. When we turned into the road leading to our house, I suddenly felt a deep, inner sadness. Tears came to my eyes and I did not dare to look at my father. We both understood. She would not be home. She would not open the door and embrace us. She would not ask how the day had been. She would not invite us to the table and pour tea in our cups. I felt an anxious tension when my father drove into the garage and we walked up to the door. Upon entering the house it was suddenly clear to us: it had become an empty house.

The large living room with the familiar paintings seemed to have turned into a waiting room the bedrooms into guest rooms, the kitchen into a cold, silent place. I wandered from room to room, and felt a shiver throughout my entire body. Everything that for years had spoken of her presence now reminded me of her absence. Everything that had always told me that she was home now told me that I would never hear her warm voice again.

I walked into her little study and saw the many family photographs. Looking at the pictures of my brothers and sister and myself which I had seen so often, I realized that they had suddenly become different pictures telling a different story. I sat at her desk and looked at some notes she had written in the days before she went to the hospital. Suddenly, I realized that she who had written me every week would never write me again. In a drawer I found my name written on folders and envelopes and realized how often she had thought about me as she sat there. Only now did I fully recognize that I had become a different man, a man without a mother, a man alone in a new way.

I asked my father, "Would you like a cup of coffee?" "I will make it," he replied. As we sat down with the cups in our hands, we felt for a moment as if we were in someone else's house.

That evening I picked up her prayerbook and asked my father, "Would you like to say the prayers I used to say with mother when I was home?" "Yes," he said, and we prayed the evening psalms which she prayed before going to bed.

During the following days things in and around the house kept reminding us of her. The time between her death and funeral became one of discovering the many ways in which she had left us. What for years had been so obvious, self-evident, and normal had now become a subject of memory. Often the small things seemed the most painful, the little customs which had become part of our life together: the way she set the table, the times she called us together for coffee, the hour she went to church. In this way, she kept dying in us every hour, every day.

When Saturday finally came, I sensed that the funeral and burial would be the first opportunity to let my mother's death become the beginning of something new, an occasion to share the first visible signs of new hope and new life. I even felt a certain joyful anticipation as I looked out over the misty fields. We would now celebrate her life, give thanks for all she had meant to us, and include the people of the village, family members, and friends in both our grief and our hope.

When the time for the service arrived, the village church was filled. Not only was every seat taken, but people were standing in the side chapels and even in the choir loft. As I entered the church and put on the vestments to preside at the service, I experienced something for which I have not yet found words.

I was about to celebrate the Eucharist for my mother, who had evoked in me the desire to become a priest and with whom I had celebrated the Eucharist innumerable times.

I was about to bless and incense her body as a last farewell to her, she who had blessed me often during her life.

I was about to announce hope and new life to all whom she had brought together here by her death, many of whom had not heard the good news of the Gospel for many years.

I was overwhelmed by the simple realization that this service, which I had dreamt about with anxious anticipation, was not an hour of fear and anxiety, but an occasion of peace and consolation. I was going to bury my own mother, speak about her to her friends, sing hymns of praise and thanksgiving to God, and offer bread and wine as signs of his enduring love for us.

The service was indeed a real celebration, just the way my father had hoped it would be. The words of the liturgy, the festive music, the songs of the congregation, and the divine gifts of the Eucharist made this a moment in which the goodness of the God of life was affirmed and our sad hearts were lifted up in gratitude.

But perhaps even more than the festive celebration in the church, the walk to the cemetery flooded us with an immense sense of God's presence. After our words and songs it was nature's turn to sing God's praise in this hour of farewell. By the time we left the church with the casket, the mist had lifted, the sun had broken through, and the green pastures were full of light. As the procession slowly found its solemn way to the cemetery, mourners became like dancers. The young horses galloping in the fields, the birds playing in the air, the poplars slowly swaying in the wind, and the cheerful sounds of children running up and down the street—all reminded us of the God of life. Even those who were still overcome by sadness and sorrow found themselves pulled away from their introspection by these unmistakable signs of nature's vitality. I had the feeling that this procession to the cemetery might be the shortest walk longest remembered.

Behind the cross walked my two nephews, little Marc and Reinier, too young to mourn but not too young to carry the bucket and the sprinkler with a sense of doing something important for their grandmother. In front of me walked the pastor of the church and my mother's oldest brother in their priestly vestments. Behind me, my brothers Paul and Wim, my brother-in-law Marc, and four neighbors carried the casket. I felt the presence of my father, my sister Laurine, my sisters-in-law Marja and Heiltjen, and Frederique my little niece. They followed the casket so closely that they could touch the flowers which covered it. As I walked I let my mother's silver rosary, which my father had given me the day before, pass through my fingers. It was hard to concentrate on anything specific. The sounds of the wind and the playful children intertwined with the sounds of the prayers arising from the long procession. It was sad and joyful, strange and familiar, old and new, serious and playful, very hard and very easy. I simply let these contrasting sensations merge in my heart and mind without trying to sort them out.

At the cemetery little more needed to be done or said. A simple prayer, a word of thanks, and a silent look at the place to which I will return many times in the years to come. My final impression was that of flowers—white flowers, yellow flowers, red flowers, and purple flowers. After everyone else had left, my father and I stood for a few moments gazing at these flowers which covered the small plot of land in which she now lay. Then and there I had to learn again that mother was dead, gone, no longer with us. Tears pushed themselves into my eyes, making me feel very alone and very sad. I could only repeat the words that have sounded through the ages: "May eternal light enlighten her that she may rest in peace."

6

hree days later I returned to the United States. Only two weeks had passed since I had left Kennedy Airport, but it seemed like ages. During the eight-hour flight I was overcome by a profound desire to sleep. The anxieties, tensions, and fears, as well as the emotions of joy, gratitude, and love had so exhausted me that I just wanted to forget everything and be carried home.

But was I going home? As I walked through the endless passageways of Kennedy Airport, waited in line for customs, and called a limousine for the trip to New Haven, I felt more like a stranger than ever. The busy scene of thousands of people coming and going was the same as always, but this time I could not help asking myself, "What am I doing here? Why do I come to this foreign country? What is it that makes me live and work so far from those who care most about me?"

It slowly dawned on me that she, who had followed every decision I made, had discussed every trip I took, had read every article and book I wrote, and had considered my life as important as hers, was no longer. Little by little I became aware that mother, although far away, had always been part of my wanderings, and that indeed I had viewed the world through the eyes of her to whom I could tell my story. I began to feel that the airport, the limousine, the long trip to my apartment, and all the other small inconveniences had become emptier, less meaningful, even somewhat absurd because the ever-present dialogue with her had suddenly come to an end. Even so, I still found myself thinking: "I should write her about this," or "She will love to hear that story when I come home for Christmas," only to realize that she would never again read my letters or hear my stories. What is the value of my trips, my lectures, my successes and failures, my struggles and joys, when my stories remain hanging in the air?

Returning to the United States was returning to my grief. Of course I have my father, and he loves me no less than my mother did. Yes, there are my brothers and sister and my many friends who surround me with their love and interest. But now, as I returned, it was her absence that pervaded my feelings, and I knew that the time had come for me to learn again how to make this world my home.

When I finally entered my room well after midnight, I looked at her portrait on the wall and noticed the many things she had given me over the last decade. I had a difficult time believing that just a few weeks ago she and my father were sitting in these chairs, talking

about all the little things by which we express our love
for each other.

The weeks that followed are hard to describe.
Fatigue, sorrow, sadness, and confusion were certainly
part of it, but also joy, gratitude, new insights, and beautiful memories. I had to fight the temptation to get back
to normal too soon. I kept thinking about Dr. Richard
Cabot who, the day after his wife died, gave a lecture as
if nothing had happened.

Indeed, I felt a certain pressure to view this as the
ideal for which to strive. But circumstances prevented
my following Cabot's example. Instead, I was able to
spend some useless time by myself. This was important,
for without it I could easily have slipped into the illu-
sion that indeed nothing has happened and nothing
has changed. In a society which is much more inclined
to help you hide your pain than to grow through it, it
is necessary to make a very conscious effort to mourn.
The days when those in grief wore dark clothes and
abstained from public life for many months are gone.
But I felt that without a very explicit discipline, I might
be tempted to return to normal and so forget my mother even against my will.

But I know that I must not forget, that I must
remember her even if remembering brings with it pain,
sorrow, and sadness. The disciples of Jesus kept themselves isolated from the people for forty days, trying
to comprehend what had happened. This long period
of mourning was necessary before they were able to

receive the Spirit. Only after this long and painful grief were they able to receive the great consolation that their Lord had promised them. For it was only after they had given up clinging to their Lord that his Spirit could descend into their hearts.

If mother's agony and death were indeed an agony and death with Christ, should I not then hope that she would also participate in the sending of the Spirit? The deeper I entered into my own grief, the more I became aware that something new was about to be born, something that I had not known before. I began to wonder if Jesus does not send his Spirit every time someone with whom we are connected by bonds of love leaves us.

To forget mother would be like forbidding her to send the Spirit to me, refusing to let her lift me up to a new level of insight and understanding of my life. I started to feel the power of Jesus' words: "It is for your own good that I am going, because unless I go, the Paraclete (the Spirit) will not come to you; but if I go, I will send him to you. . . . When the Spirit of truth comes he will lead you to the complete truth" (Jn 16:7,13).

Is it for my own good that Jesus died, that my friends and relatives died, that my mother died? Am I able to affirm with my entire being that in and through Christ's death the Spirit of truth comes to us? Must I grieve and mourn so that I will be ready to receive the Spirit when he comes?

These questions became very real to me in those confusing weeks after mother's death. I said to myself,

"This is a time of waiting for the Spirit of truth to come, and woe unto me if, by forgetting her, I prevent her from doing God's work in me." I sensed that something much more than a filial act of remembering was at stake, much more than an honoring of my dead mother, much more than a holding on to her beautiful example. Very specifically, what was at stake was the life of the Spirit in me. To remember her does not mean telling her story over and over again to my friends, nor does it mean pictures on the wall or a stone on her grave; it does not even mean constantly thinking about her. No. It means making her a participant in God's ongoing work of redemption by allowing her to dispel in me a little more of my darkness and lead me a little closer to the light. In those weeks of mourning she died in me more and more every day, making it impossible for me to cling to her as my mother. Yet, by letting her go, I did not lose her. Rather, I found that she is closer to me than ever. In and through the Spirit of Christ, she indeed is becoming a part of my very being.

Conclusion

I am back at work now: teaching, reading, writing, laughing, and getting angry. It all seems the same as five weeks ago. But things are not the same. Mother has died and it was for my own good that she left. I speak less and less about her, even my thoughts are less involved with her—yet I have not forgotten her. Remembering her now means a greater willingness to receive the Spirit of truth and to see more clearly my own vocation.

There is so much darkness to be dispelled, so much deceit to be unmasked, and so many ambiguities to be resolved. Mother's death is God's way of converting me, of letting his Spirit set me free. It is all still very new. A great deal has happened in these weeks, but what will happen in the months and years ahead will be far more than I can now understand. I am still waiting, yet already receiving; still hoping, yet already possessing; still wondering, yet already knowing.

Sometimes I find myself daydreaming about radical changes, new beginnings and great conversions. Yet

I know that I must be patient and allow her who taught me so much by her life to teach me even more by her death.

A Letter of
Consolation

Introduction

This letter was written six months after the death of my mother. I wrote it to my father as a letter of consolation. When I wrote it I did not think of making it public, but now, three years later, I feel a certain urge to do so. Because now I have a real desire to offer this letter to all those who suffer the pain that death can bring and who search for new life. During the last few years I have come to realize in a new way what it means to live and die for each other. As this awareness grew in me, I began to wonder if the fruits of our grief are to be tasted only by ourselves.

Like other letters, this letter has its own history and I would like to introduce its publication by offering some explanation of why I decided to write it.

Very shortly after my mother's funeral in October 1978, I returned from Holland to the United States. A few days later I was busy again, as always, teaching, counseling students, attending faculty meetings, answering mail, and doing the many things that fill the daily life of a university teacher. There had been little or no opportunity to let mother's suffering and death enter deeply into my innermost self.

During the days that my mother was dying and during the days immediately after her death, I tried to pay as much attention as I could to my family and to anyone who offered friendship and love. And then, back in the United States, far away from home, the busy school life certainly did not encourage me to listen to my own inner cries. But one day, when I paused for a while in my office between appointments, I suddenly realized that I had not shed a single tear before or after mother's death. At that moment I saw that the world had such a grasp on me that it did not allow me to fully experience even the most personal, the most intimate, and the most mysterious event of my life. It seemed as if the voices around me were saying, "You have to keep going. Life goes on; people die, but you must continue to live, to work, to struggle. The past cannot be recreated. Look at what is ahead." I was obedient to these voices: I gave my lectures with the same enthusiasm as ever; I listened to students and their problems as if nothing had happened; and I worked with the same compulsiveness that had characterized my life since I started to teach. But I knew then that this would not last if I really took my mother and myself seriously. By a happy coincidence—no, by a gracious gift of God—I had planned a six months' retreat with the Trappist monks at the Abbey of the Genesee, which during the past years had become a second home to me.

When I arrived at the monastery in January I knew that this was going to be my time of grief. On several occasions, while sitting in my little room surrounded by the deep silence of the monastery, I noticed tears coming from my eyes. I did not really understand this. I was not thinking about mother, I was not remembering her illness, her death, or her funeral, but from a place in me deeper than I could reach, grief welled up and manifested itself in soft weeping.

As the days and weeks passed I experienced a growing urge to live through more fully and more directly the loss of which my tears reminded me. But I did not want to do this alone. I wanted to do it with someone who could really understand what was happening inside me. And who could better understand me than my own father? It was an obvious and easy decision, because ever since my mother's death his letters had become my greatest source of comfort. In these letters he had told me about his own grief and his struggle to build a new, meaningful life without her. Maybe I could offer him consolation and comfort by uniting my pain with his.

Thus, I started to write this letter to my father, a letter to speak with him about her whom we had both loved so much, a letter to show him my love and affection, a letter to offer him some of my reflections on mother's death—in short, a letter of consolation. I wrote and wrote and wrote. Once I started to write I realized how much I felt, how much I wanted to say, and how much had remained hidden during the six months since mother had died.

To whom did I write this letter? To my father, surely. But I was also writing to myself. Who was consoled? My father was, I know, but when I finally wrote down the last words, I knew that I had received as much and maybe more comfort and consolation than he would. Many letters are that way: they touch the writer as much as the receiver.

I now realize that this letter had to be written for my father, for me, and maybe, too, for many others who are asking the same questions that we were asking. When I asked my father, two and a half years after the letter was written, how he would feel about making it available to others in the form of a small book, he said, "If you think that your writing about mother's death and about our grief can be a source of hope and consolation to more people than just ourselves, do not be afraid to have it printed."

And thus, after some thought and much encouragement from friends, I felt that it would be good to take the letter out of the privacy of my life and that of my father and offer it to those who know the same darkness and are searching for the same light.

I hope and pray that I made the right decision.

HENRI J.M. NOUWEN
December 29, 1981

Dear Father

*N*ext Monday it will be half a year since mother died. It will be Holy Week and both of us will be preparing ourselves to celebrate Easter. How will this Easter be for us? You will be in the parish church of our little Dutch town listening to the story of Christ's resurrection. I will read that same story to monks and guests in a Trappist monastery in upstate New York. Both of us will look at the Easter candle, symbol of the risen Christ, and think not only of him but also of her. Our minds and hearts will be flooded with ideas and feelings that are too deep, too complex, and too intimate to express. But I am sure that we both shall think about last year's Easter, when she was still with us. We both shall remember how she loved this great feast and how she decorated the house with flowers and the dinner table with purple and yellow ribbons. Somehow it seems long, long ago. Isn't that your experience also?

The last six months could as well have been six years. Her death changed our experience of time; the short period between last October and this April seemed a very strange time in which the days, weeks, and months were as long as they are for a small child who is taking his first steps. We had to relearn life. Every "normal" experience became for us like a new experience. It had the quality of a "first time." How often have we used these words! The first Christmas without mother, the first New Year without mother, the first wedding anniversary without mother. And now it will be the first Easter without mother. I know that you have been asking yourself often, as I have, "How will it be without her?" We can hardly remember any of these events without her being part of them. We can no longer predict how we will feel on these familiar days and occasions. They are, in fact, no longer familiar. They have become unknown to us. We have become suddenly aware how intimately our ideas, feelings, and perceptions were determined by her presence. Easter was not only an important day to celebrate, but a day to celebrate with her, a day on which her voice was heard, her letters anticipated, her active presence felt—so much so that we could not distinguish between the joys brought to us by the feast and the joys brought to us by her presence at the feast. They had become one and the same. But now we are forced to make a distinction, and now we have become like children who have to learn to do things for the first time on their own.

New experiences such as these have made the last six months a strange time for us. Her death became an ongoing death for us. Every time we lived through another event without her, we felt her absence in a new way. We became aware of deep connections with her that we had forgotten for a while but that were brought back to consciousness by the forward movement of history. And each time, she died again in us. Memories of what she would have done, said, or written on certain occasions made us more aware of her not being with us and deepened our grief.

Real grief is not healed by time. It is false to think that the passing of time will slowly make us forget her and take away our pain. I really want to console you in this letter, but not by suggesting that time will take away your pain, and that in one, two, three, or more years you will not miss her so much anymore. I would not only be telling a lie, I would be diminishing the importance of mother's life, underestimating the depth of your grief, and mistakenly relativizing the power of the love that has bound mother and you together for forty-seven years. If time does anything, it deepens our grief. The longer we live, the more fully we become aware of who she was for us, and the more intimately we experience what her love meant for us. Real, deep love is, as you know, very unobtrusive, seemingly easy and obvious, and so present that we take it for granted. Therefore, it is often only in retrospect—or better, in memory—that we fully realize its power and depth. Yes, indeed, love often makes itself visible in pain. The pain we are now experiencing shows us how deep, full, intimate, and all-pervasive her love was.

Is this a consolation? Does this bring comfort? It appears that I am doing the opposite of bringing consolation. Maybe so. Maybe these words will only increase your tears and deepen your grief. But for me, your son, who grieves with you, there is no other way. I want to comfort and console you, but not in a way that covers up real pain and avoids all wounds. I am writing you this letter in the firm conviction that reality can be faced and entered with an open mind and an open heart, and in the sincere belief that consolation and comfort are to be found where our wounds hurt most.

When I write to you, therefore, that, in our remembering, not only the full depth of mother's love but also the full pain of her leaving us will become known to us, I do so with the trying question in mind: "Why is it that she died before we did and why is it that we are the ones who have to carry the burden of grief?" You must have asked yourself this question many times. You have lived your life with the unquestioned assumption that you would die before mother. You felt this way not simply because you were three years older than she or because her health always seemed better than yours, but because you sensed that she would be more capable of living on without you than you without her. Why then are you the one who has to relearn life without her, and why are you the one who came to know her not only in the joy of her presence but in the pain of her absence? She has been spared the sorrow of your death; she never had to experience life without you. All the sorrow has been given to you to bear, and you have been entrusted with that awesome task of discovering her love not only in life but in death. Why? Although I am twenty-nine years younger than you are, and although the "logic of life" says parents die before their children, for me the question is no different, because love does not know "clock time."

I am writing this letter to you conscious of this great question. I want to explore with you and for you the meaning of her death and our life, of her life and our death. In your letters to me since her death—letters richer and fuller than any you wrote to me before—you have raised the question of death yourself. Ever since we saw her still face in the hospital, we have wondered what death really is. It is a question mother has left us with, and we want to face it, enter it, explore it, and let it grow in us. By doing so we may be able to console one another. It will be a hard road to travel, but if we travel it together we may have less to fear. I am glad, therefore, that in this quiet and peaceful Trappist monastery I have the opportunity to write you this letter, and I am especially glad that I can write to you during the days when both of us are preparing ourselves to celebrate the resurrection of our Lord Jesus Christ.

1

*O*ften I feel sad about the great distance between us.
Although I have always been content with living
in the United States, since mother's death I have sensed
more than before the distance that prevents me from
being of more help and support to you during these
difficult months. Regular letters and occasional phone
calls are a very limited substitute for being together. And
yet the paradox of it all is that the distance between us
may prove after all to be a blessing in disguise. If I were
still living in Holland and were able to visit you every
weekend and call you every day, I should probably never
have been able to let you know my deeper feelings about
mother and you. Isn't it true that it is much harder to
say deep things to each other than to write them? Isn't
it much more frightening to express our deeper feelings about each other when we sit around the breakfast
table than when the Atlantic Ocean separates us? We
have spent many hours watching television together
since mother died. We have often had a meal together
at home or in a restaurant. We have taken little rides

together through the woods. But seldom, very seldom, have we spoken about what was closest to our hearts. It was as if the physical closeness prevented the spiritual closeness we both desired. I am not sure if I fully understand this myself, but it seems that we are not the only people for whom this holds true. Physical and spiritual closeness are two quite different things, and they can—although they do not always—inhibit each other. The great distance between us may be enabling us to develop a relationship that you might not be able to develop with your other children and their families who live so close to you.

One obvious result of our distance is that you have started to write letters to me. Since mother died you not only write more often, but your letters are different. That has meant a lot to me during the last six months. I had become so used to mother's weekly letters, in which she told about all the family events, big and small, and kept showing her interest in my own life with all its ups and downs, that I feared their sudden absence. You used to write very seldom, and when you did, your letters consisted mostly of general, almost philosophical, reflections; they did not reveal much about your actual work, concerns, or feelings. It always seemed as though you felt that mother was the one who took care of personal relationships. I remember how often you used to say, as I left the house to return to the United States, "Don't forget to write mother." It was almost as if you were not very interested in hearing from me and were primarily concerned that mother and I would stay in close touch. I do not think that this was true. On the contrary, I think that you were very interested in hearing from me, but you usually left it to mother to express the affection, concern, and interest that you shared with her. Sometimes it was even humorous. Whenever I called you by phone, I was surprised that you took it for granted that I really called for mother. I always had the hardest time keeping you on the line for more than a few seconds. After reassuring me that everything was fine with you, you always said quickly, "Well, here's mother." I knew a call made you happy, but your happiness seemed to be derived from mother's joy and gratefulness.

But now she is no longer there for you to hide behind. And you have indeed stepped forward! You have written me letters as warm and personal as those of mother. In fact, even more so. And just as I once looked forward to receiving mother's letters, I now long for yours. Now I not only know—as I did before—that you are interested in my life, but I can also see it expressed in your written words. And now you accept the simple and true fact that I write to you for yourself alone and call you for yourself alone.

The more I think about this, the more I realize that mother's death caused you to step forward in a way you could not before. Maybe there is even more to say than that. Maybe I have to say that you have found in yourself the capacity to be not only a father, but a mother as well. You have found in yourself that same gift of compassion that brought mother so much love and so much suffering. You have started to see more clearly the loneliness of your friends and to sympathize more with their search for company; you have begun to feel more deeply the fears of your widowed colleagues and to experience more sharply the mystery of death. And—if I may say so—you have discovered that you have a son who has been alone since he left your house. Becoming a priest for me has in fact meant to enter the road of "the long loneliness," as Dorothy Day called it, and my many physical and spiritual journeys have deepened that experience even further. That long loneliness is what had made me feel so especially close to mother and has made me feel so lost by her death. But isn't this now also the basis for a unique solidarity between the two of us? Am I right when I suppose that you, who are known and feared for your irony and sarcasm, for your sharp wit and critical analysis—all qualities that made you such a good lawyer—are now allowing your tender side to come more to the center and are now experiencing a new bond with those who are dear to you?

There is always that strange tendency in marriage to divide roles, even psychological roles. And our culture certainly encourages that: mother for the children, you for earning a living; mother to be gentle and forgiving, you to be strict and demanding; mother hospitable and receptive, you reserved and selective. In fact, you even liked to play with these differences and point them out in your comments at dinner. But now there are no longer any qualities to divide, and you are challenged to let develop more fully in yourself what you so admired in mother. I even sense that the memory of mother, and the way she lived her life with you, makes you consciously desire to let her qualities remain visible for your children and your friends—visible in you.

You are not imitating mother. You are not saying, "I will do things the way mother used to do them." That would be artificial and certainly not an honor to her. No, you are becoming more yourself, you are exploring those areas of life that always were part of you but remained somewhat dormant in mother's presence. I think that we both have a new and honorable task. It is the task to be father, son, and friend in a new way, a way that mother made possible not only through her life, but through her death. When Jesus said that if a grain of wheat dies it will yield a rich harvest, he not only spoke about his own death but indicated the new meaning he would give to our death. So we have to ask ourselves, "Where do we see the harvest of mother's death?" There is no doubt in my mind that this harvest is becoming visible first of all in those who loved her most. Our deep love for her allows us to be the first to reap the harvest and to share with others the gifts of her death.

Isn't it here that we have to start if we want to discover the meaning of mother's death? Before anything else, we have to come into touch with—yes, even claim—the mysterious reality of new life in ourselves.

Others might see it, feel it, and enjoy it before we do. That is why I am writing to you about it. We may help each other to see this new life. That would be true consolation. It would make us experience in the center of our beings that the pain mother's death caused us has led us to a new way of being, in which the distance between mother, father, or child slowly dissolves. Thus our separation from mother brings us to a new inner unity and invites us to make that new unity a source of joy and hope for each other and for others as well.

2

As I said earlier, mother's death has made us raise more directly and explicitly the question of death itself. The question about death, however, is mostly asked by someone who is himself not dying. You yourself made me aware of this when you reminded me how much mother spoke about her death when there was no real danger and yet hardly mentioned it at all when she was actually dying. It seems indeed important that we face death before we are in any real danger of dying and reflect on our mortality before all our conscious and unconscious energy is directed to the struggle to survive. It is important to be prepared for death, very important; but if we start thinking about it only when we are terminally ill, our reflections will not give us the support we need. We enjoy good health now. We are asking about death, mother's death and our own, not because we are dying, but because we feel strong enough to raise the question about our most basic human infirmity.

I want to take up the challenge of this question. This indeed seems to be the opportune time not only for you, but also for me. We both have to ask ourselves what mother's death means, and we both are confronted in a new way with our own deaths. The fact that you are "already" seventy-six and I am "only" forty-seven is not a real hindrance to a common meditation on death. I think, in fact, that mother's death has taken away much of the age difference between us, so that the prospect of dying and death is not really different for you and for me. Once you have reached the top of the mountain, it does not make much difference at which point on the way down you take a picture of the valley—as long as you are not in the valley itself.

I think, then, that our first task is to befriend death. I like that expression "to befriend." I first heard it used by Jungian analyst James Hillman when he attended a seminar I taught on Christian Spirituality at Yale Divinity School. He emphasized the importance of "befriending": befriending your dreams, befriending your shadow, befriending your unconscious. He made it convincingly clear that in order to become full human beings, we have to claim the totality of our experience; we come to maturity by integrating not only the light but also the dark side of our story into our selfhood. That made a lot of sense to me, since I am quite familiar with my own inclination, and that of others, to avoid, deny, or suppress the painful side of life, a tendency that always leads to physical, mental, or spiritual disaster.

And isn't death, the frightening unknown that lurks in the depths of our unconscious minds, like a great shadow that we perceive only dimly in our dreams? Befriending death seems to be the basis of all other forms of befriending. I have a deep sense, hard to articulate, that if we could really befriend death we would be free people. So many of our doubts and hesitations, ambivalences and insecurities are bound up with our deep-seated fear of death that our lives would be significantly different if we could relate to death as a familiar guest instead of a threatening stranger.

In the book *Nacht und Nebel*, the Dutchman Floris Bakels writes about his experiences in the German prisons and concentration camps of the Second World War. He makes very clear what power a man can have who has befriended his own death. I know how much this book has moved you, and I was very happy with the copy I just received. Wouldn't you say that Floris Bakels was able to survive the horrors of Dachau and other camps and write about it thirty-two years later precisely because he had befriended death? It seems, at least to me, that Floris Bakels said in many different ways to his SS captors, "You have no power over me, because I have already died." Fear of death often drives us into death, but by befriending death, we can face our mortality and choose life freely.

But how do we befriend death? During the last few years you have seen many deaths—even of people you knew quite well. They have touched you, shocked you, surprised you, and even caused you grief, but when mother died it seemed as if death came to you for the first time. Why? I think because love—deep, human love—does not know death. The way you and mother had become one, and the way this oneness had deepened itself during forty-seven years of marriage, did not allow termination. Real love says, "Forever." Love will always reach out toward the eternal. Love comes from that place within us where death cannot enter. Love does not accept the limits of hours, days, weeks, months, years, or centuries. Love is not willing to be imprisoned by time.

That is why mother's death was such a totally different experience for you from the deaths of so many other people you have known. In the core of your being, you—your love—could not accept her leaving you so drastically, so radically, so totally, and so irretrievably. Her death went directly against your most profound intuitions. And so I could well understand your writing to me that mother's death had led you to the general question of death's meaning. Someone might say, "Why did it take him so long to raise that question? He is seventy-six years old—and only now does he wonder about the meaning of death." But someone who says this does not understand that only mother could raise that question for you, because in her dying the real absurdity of death revealed itself to you. Only her death could really make you protest in your innermost being and make you cry out, "Why could our love not prevent her from dying?"

Yet, the same love that reveals the absurdity of death also allows us to befriend death. The same love that forms the basis of our grief is also the basis of our hope; the same love that makes us cry out in pain also must enable us to develop a liberating intimacy with our own most basic brokenness. Without faith, this must sound like a contradiction. But our faith in him whose love overcame death and who rose from the grave on the third day converts this contradiction into a paradox, the most healing paradox of our existence. Floris Bakels experienced this in a unique way. He came to see and feel that the power of love is stronger than the power of death and that it is indeed true that "God is love." Surrounded by people dying from hunger, torture, and total exhaustion, and knowing quite well that any hour could be his hour to die, he found in the core of his being a love so strong and so profound that the fear of death lost its power over him. For Floris Bakels, this love was not a general feeling or emotion, nor an idea about a benevolent Supreme Being. No, it was the very concrete, real, and intimate love of Jesus Christ, Son of God and redeemer of the world. With his whole being he knew that he was loved with an infinite love, held in an eternal embrace and surrounded by an unconditional care. This love was so concrete, so tangible, so direct, and so close for him that the temptation to interpret this religious experience as the fantasy of a starved mind had no lasting hold on him. The more deeply and fully he experienced Christ's love, the more he came to see that the many loves in his life—the love of his parents, his brother and sisters, his wife, and his friends—were reflections of the great "first" love of God.

I am convinced that it was the deeply felt love of God—felt in and through Jesus Christ—that allowed Floris Bakels to face his own death and the deaths of others so directly. It was this love that gave him the freedom and energy to help people in agony and made it possible for him to resume a normal life after he returned from the hell of Dachau.

I am writing so much about Bakels because I know that you, being of the same generation and the same profession, can understand him quite well and will lend him a sympathetic ear. He can indeed show you better than psychologists or psychoanalysts what it means to befriend death.

Although you and I also tasted the terror of the Nazis, you as a young man who had to hide yourself to escape from deportation and I as a fearful child, and although we all had to struggle hard to keep alive during the horrible "winter of hunger" in 1944–45, we were spared the horrors of the concentration camps and did not have to face death in the way Floris Bakels did. Thus, we were not forced to befriend death at such an early age. But mother's death invites us to do so now. Many people seem never to befriend death and die as if they were losing a hopeless battle. But we do not have to share that sad fate. Mother's death can bring us that freedom of which Bakels writes; it can make us deeply aware that her love was a reflection of a love that does not and cannot die—the love that we both will affirm again on Easter Sunday.

3

*I*n no way do I want to suggest that you have been repressing or denying your mortality. In fact, I know few people who have been so open about their own death. At different times you have spoken about your own death publicly and privately, to strangers and to friends, mockingly and seriously. Sometimes you even embarrassed mother and your guests with your directness! I remember your mentioning on several occasions how quickly our "great lives" are forgotten and how short-lived are the pious memories of our friends and colleagues. I remember how you told me, before you left on a long trip to Brazil, what I should do in case a fatal accident took the lives of you both. And I remember your very concrete wishes about the way you hoped your children and friends would respond to your death. Sometimes your words about your death had a sarcastic quality, and conveyed a desire to unmask sentimentalism and false romanticism. You even enjoyed gently shocking the pious feelings of your friends and testing your and their sense of reality. But mostly, your words were serious and showed that you were indeed reflecting on the end of your own life. Thus it is quite clear that you have not been living as if your life would go on forever. You are too intelligent and too realistic for that.

Still, hidden in us there are levels of not-knowing, not-understanding and not-feeling that can only be revealed to us in our moments of great crisis. For some people such moments never come, for others they come frequently. For some they come early, for others they come quite late. We might think that we have a certain insight into "what life is all about" until an unexpected crisis throws us off balance and forces us to rethink our most basic presuppositions. In fact, we never really know how deeply our lives are anchored, and the experience of crisis can open up dimensions of life that we never knew existed.

Mother's death is certainly one of the most crucial experiences of both our lives, perhaps even the most crucial. Before her death, it was impossible to know even vaguely what it would do to us. Now we are beginning to sense its impact. Gradually we are able to see where it is leading us. A new confrontation with death is taking place, a confrontation that we could never have created ourselves. Whatever we felt, said, or thought about death in the past was always within the reach of our own emotional or intellectual capacities. In a certain sense, it remained within the range of our own influence and control. Remarks and ideas about our own deaths remained *our* remarks and *our* ideas and were therefore subject to our own inventiveness and originality. But mother's death was totally outside the field of our control or influence. It left us powerless. When we saw how slowly she lost contact with us and fell away from us, we could do nothing but stand beside her bed and watch death exercise its ruthless power. This experience is not an experience for which we can really prepare ourselves. It is so new and so overpowering that all of our previous speculations and reflections seem trivial and superficial in the presence of the awesome reality of death. Thus mother's death changes the question of death into a new question. It opens us to levels of life that could not have been reached before, even if we had had the desire to reach them.

What did mother's death do to you? I do not know and cannot know since it is something so intimate that nobody can enter fully into your emotions. But if your experience of her death is in any way close to mine, you were "invited"—as I was—to re-evaluate your whole life. Mother's death made you stop and look back in a way you had not done before. Suddenly you entered into a situation that made you see your many years of life—your life as a student, a young professional, a successful lawyer, a well-known professor—with a bird's-eye view. I remember your telling me how you could capture your long and complex history in one clear picture, and how from the point of view of mother's death, your life lost much of its complexity and summarized itself in a few basic lines. In that way her death gave you new eyes with which to see your own life and helped you to distinguish between the many accidental aspects and the few essential elements.

Death indeed simplifies; death does not tolerate endless shadings and nuances. Death lays bare what really matters, and in this way becomes your judge. It seems that we both have experienced this after mother's death and funeral. During the last six months we have been reviewing our life with mother. For you this meant opening drawers that had not been opened for years; looking at photographs whose very existence you had forgotten; reading old letters now yellow and wrinkled with age; and picking up books that had collected much dust on the shelves. For me this meant re-reading her letters to me; looking again at the gifts she brought to me on visits; and praying with renewed attention the psalms we so often prayed together. Long-forgotten events returned to memory as if they had taken place only recently. It seemed as if we could put our whole lives in the palms of our hands like small precious stones and gaze at them with tenderness and admiration. How tiny, how beautiful, how valuable!

I think that from the point of view of mother's death and our own mortality, we can now see our lives as a long process of mortification. You are familiar with that word. Priests use it a lot during Lent. They say, "You have to mortify yourself." It sounds unpleasant and harsh and moralistic. But mortification—literally, "making death"—is what life is all about, a slow discovery of the mortality of all that is created so that we can appreciate its beauty without clinging to it as if it were a lasting possession. Our lives can indeed be seen as a process of becoming familiar with death, as a school in the art of dying. I do not mean this in a morbid way. On the contrary, when we see life constantly relativized by death, we can enjoy it for what it is: a free gift. The pictures, letters, and books of the past reveal life to us as a constant saying of farewell to beautiful places, good people, and wonderful experiences. Look at the pictures of your children when you could play with them on the floor of the living room. How quickly you had to say goodbye to them! Look at the snapshots of your bike trips with mother in Brittany in the midthirties. How few were the summers in which those trips were possible! Read mother's letters when you were in Amalfi recuperating from your illness and my letters to you from my first trip to England. They speak now of fleeting moments. Look at the wedding pictures of your children and at the Bible I gave you on the day of my ordination. All these times have passed by like friendly visitors, leaving you with dear memories but also with the sad recognition of the shortness of life. In every arrival there is a leavetaking; in every reunion there is a separation; in each one's growing up there is a growing old; in every smile there is a tear; and in every success there is a loss. All living is dying and all celebration is mortification too.

Although this was happening all the time during our rich and varied lives, we did not notice it with the same acuteness as we do now. There was so much life, so much vitality, and so much exuberance that the presence of death was less striking and was only acknowledged in the way we acknowledge our shadows on a sunny day. There were moments of pain, sadness, disillusionment; there were illnesses, setbacks, conflicts, and worries. But they came and went like the seasons of the year, and the forces of life always proved victorious. Then mother died. Her death was a definitive end, a total break that presented itself with a finality unlike any other. For a while, we kept living as if she were only gone for a time and could return at any moment. We even kept doing things as if we were preparing for the moment when she would appear again on our doorsteps. But as the days passed, our hearts came to know that she was gone, never to return. And it was then that real grief began to invade us. It was then that we turned to the past and saw that death had been present in our lives all along and that the many farewells and goodbyes had been pointing to this dark hour. And it was then that we raised in a wholly new way the question of the meaning of death.

4

*W*hen we experienced the deep loss at mother's death, we also experienced our total inability to do anything about it. We, who loved mother so much and would have done anything possible to alleviate her pain and agony, could do absolutely nothing. All of us who stood around her bed during her last days felt powerless. Sometimes we looked at the doctors and nurses with the vain hope that maybe *they* could change the course of events, but we realized that what we were witnessing was the inevitable reality of death, a reality we shall all have to face one day soon.

I think it is important for us to allow this experience of powerlessness in the face of mother's death to enter deeply into our souls, because it holds the key to a deeper understanding of the meaning of death.

Father, you are a man with a strong personality, a powerful will, and a convincing sense of self. You are known as a hard worker, a persistent fighter for your clients, and a man who never loses an argument, or at least will never confess to losing one! You have achieved what you strove for. Your successful career has rewarded your efforts richly and has strengthened you in your conviction that success in life is the result of hard work. If anything is clear about your life-style, it is that you want to keep your hands on the tiller of your ship. You like to be in control, able to make your own decisions and direct your own course. Experience has taught you that displaying weakness does not create respect and that it is safer to bear your burden in secret than to ask for pity. You never strove for power and influence, and even refused many positions that would have given you national recognition, but you fiercely guarded your own spiritual, mental, and economic autonomy. Not only did you in fact achieve an impressive amount of autonomy for yourself, but you also encouraged your children to become free and independent people as soon as possible. I think it was this great value you put on autonomy that made you proud to see me leave for the United States. I am sure you did not want me to be so far from home, but this inconvenience was richly compensated for by the joy you drew from my ability to "make it" independently of the support of my family and friends. One of your most often repeated remarks to me and to my brothers and sister was, "Be sure not to become dependent on the power, influence, or money of others. Your freedom to make your own decisions is your greatest possession. Do not ever give that up."

This attitude—an attitude greatly admired by mother and all of us in the family—explains why anything that reminded you of death threatened you. You found it very hard to be ill, you were usually a bit irritated with the illnesses of others, and you had very little sympathy for people whom you considered "failures." The weak did not attract you.

Mother's death opened up for you a dimension of life in which the key word is not autonomy, but surrender. In a very deep and existential way, her death was a frontal attack on your feeling of autonomy and independence, and in this sense, a challenge to conversion, that is, to the profound turning around of your priorities. I am not saying that mother's death made your autonomy and independence less valuable, but only that it put them into a new framework, the framework of life as a process of detachment.

Autonomy and detachment are not necessarily opposites. They can be if they confront each other on the same level of existence. But I sincerely believe that a healthy autonomy can give you the real strength to detach yourself when it is necessary to do so. Let me try to explain what I mean.

Even when we are trying to be in control and to determine our own course in life, we have to admit that life remains the great unknown to us. Although you worked quite hard in life to build up a successful career and to give your family a happy home, some of the main factors that made things develop the way they did were totally out of your hands. Many things that happened *to* you were as important as the things that happened *through* you. Fifty years ago, neither you nor anyone else could have predicted your present situation. And how futile it is for us to predict our own immediate or distant future. Things that made us worry greatly later prove to be quite insignificant, and things to which we hardly gave a thought before they took place turn our lives around. Thus our autonomy is rooted in unknown soil. This constitutes the great challenge: to be so free that we can be obedient, to be so autonomous that we can be dependent, to be so in control that we can surrender ourselves. Here we touch the great paradox in life: to live in order to be able to die. That is what detachment is all about. Detachment is not the opposite of autonomy but its fruit. It takes a good driver to know when to use his brakes!

This is far from theoretical, as you well know. We have both seen how some of our friends could not accept unforeseen changes in their lives and were unable to deal with an unknown future. When things went differently than they had expected or took a drastic turn, they did not know how to adjust to the new situation. Sometimes they became bitter and sour. Often they clung to familiar patterns of living that were no longer adequate and kept repeating what once made sense but no longer could speak to the real circumstances of the moment. Death has often affected people in this way, as we know too well. The death of husband, wife, child, or friend can cause people to stop living toward the unknown future and make them withdraw into the familiar past. They keep holding on to a few precious memories and customs and see their lives as having come to a standstill. They start to live as if they were thinking, "For me it is all over. There is nothing more to expect from life." As you can see, here the opposite of detachment is taking place; here is a re-attachment that makes life stale and takes all vitality out of existence. It is a life in which hope no longer exists.

If mother's death were to lead us onto that road, her death would have no real meaning for us. Her death would be or become for us a death that closes the future and makes us live the rest of our lives in the enclosure of our own past. Then, our experience of powerlessness would not give us the freedom to detach ourselves from the past, but would imprison us in our own memories and immobilize us. Thus we would also lose the autonomy you have always held so dear.

I think there is a much more human option. It is the option to re-evaluate the past as a continuing challenge to surrender ourselves to an unknown future. It is the option to understand our experience of powerlessness as an experience of being guided, even when we do not know exactly where. Remember what Jesus said to Peter when he appeared to him after his resurrection: "When you were young you put on your own belt and walked where you liked; but when you grow old you will stretch out your hands, and somebody else will put a belt round you and take you where you would rather not go." Jesus said this immediately after he had told Peter three times to look after his sheep. Here we can see that a growing surrender to the unknown is a sign of spiritual maturity and does not take away autonomy. Mother's death is indeed an invitation to surrender ourselves more freely to the future, in the conviction that one of the most important parts of our lives may still be ahead of us and that mother's life and death were meant to make this possible. Do not forget that only after Jesus' death could his disciples fulfill their vocation.

I am constantly struck by the fact that those who are most detached from life, those who have learned through living that there is nothing and nobody in this life to cling to, are the really creative people. They are free to move constantly away from the familiar, safe places and can keep moving forward to new, unexplored areas of life. I am not suggesting to you that you are called to do something unusual or spectacular in your old age—although there is no telling to what you might be called! But I am thinking primarily of a spiritual process by which we can live our lives more freely than before, more open to God's guidance and more willing to respond when he speaks to our innermost selves.

Mother's death encourages us to give up the illusions of immortality we might still have and to experience in a new way our total dependence on God's love, a dependence that does not take away our free selfhood but purifies and ennobles it. Here you may catch a glimpse of the answer to the question of why mother died before you and why you have been given new years to live. Now you can say things to yourself, to others, and to God that were not disclosed to you before.

5

*I*n all the previous reflections, dear father, an idea has emerged that was only vaguely in my mind when I started to write. It is the idea that the meaning of death is not so much the meaning our death has for us as the meaning it has for others. That explains why the meaning of mother's death and the meaning of our death are so closely related. I have a feeling that to the degree we can experience the fact that mother died for you, for her children, and for many others, our own death will have more meaning for us. I will try to explain this to you in such a way that you can find a certain obviousness in this idea.

Let me start with your own observation, which you have often made since mother's death, namely, that she lived her life for others. The more you reflected on her life, looked at her portraits, read her letters, and listened to what others said about her, the more you realized how her whole life was lived in the service of other people. I too am increasingly impressed by her attentiveness to the needs of others. This attitude was so much a part of her that it hardly seems remarkable. Only now can we see its full power and beauty. She rarely asked attention for herself. Her interest and attention went out to the needs and concerns of others. She was open to those who came to her. Many found it easy to talk with her about themselves and remarked how much at ease they had felt in her presence. This was especially noticeable during her visits to me in the United States. Often she knew my students better after one evening than I did after a year, and for many years to come she would keep asking about them. During the last six months I have grown painfully aware of how accustomed I had become to her unceasing interest in all that I did, felt, thought, or wrote, and how much I had taken it for granted that, even if nobody else cared, she certainly did. The absence of that caring attention often gives me a deep feeling of loneliness. I know that this is even truer for you. You no longer hear her ask how well you slept, what your plans are for the day, or what you are writing about. You no longer hear her advise you to be careful on the road, to eat more, or to get some extra sleep. All these simple but so supportive and healing ways of caring are no longer there, and in their absence we begin to feel more and more what it means to be alone.

What I want to say now, however, is that she who lived for others also died for others. Her death should not be seen as a sudden end to all her care, as a great halt to her receptivity to others. There are people who experience the death of someone they love as a betrayal. They feel rejected, left alone, and even fooled. They seem to say to their husband, wife, or friend, "How could you do this to me? Why did you leave me behind in this way? I never bargained for this!" Sometimes people even feel angry toward those who die, and express this by a paralyzing grief, by a regression to a state of total dependence, by all sorts of illnesses and complaints, and even by dying themselves.

If, however, mother's life was indeed a life lived for us, we must be willing to accept her death as a death for us, a death that is not meant to paralyze us, make us totally dependent, or provide an excuse for all sorts of complaints, but a death that should make us stronger, freer, and more mature. To say it even more drastically: we must have the courage to believe that her death was good for us and that she died so that we might live. This is quite a radical viewpoint and it might offend the sensitivities of some people. Why? Because, in fact, I am saying, "It is good for us that she left us, and to the extent that we do not accept this we have not yet fully understood the meaning of her life." This might sound harsh and even offensive, but I believe deeply that it is true. Indeed, I believe even more deeply that we will come to experience this ourselves.

Although the time is past when widows were burned with their dead husbands—even a contemporary Phileas Fogg would not encounter such a scene on a trip around the world—still, in a psychological sense, many widows and widowers end their lives with that of their spouse. They respond to the death of husband or wife with a sudden lack of vitality and behavior that turns life into a gruesome waiting room for death. I am aware of the fact that the other extreme—living on as if one had never been married—can also be seen. But since that is not within the horizon of your capacities, I do not need to talk about that here. What is important for us to recognize is that mother's own life invites us to see her death as a death that can bring us not only grief but also joy, not only pain but also healing, not only the experience of having lost but also the experience of having found.

This viewpoint is not just my personal viewpoint as against the viewpoint of others. It is the Christian viewpoint, that is, a viewpoint based on the life and death and resurrection of Jesus Christ. I need to be very clear about this, or you might not really understand what I am trying to express.

Five days have passed since I began this letter and it is now the evening before Holy Thursday. During this Holy Week we are confronted with death more than during any other season of the liturgical year. We are called to meditate not just on death in general or on our own death in particular, but on the death of Jesus Christ who is God and man. We are challenged to look at him dying on a cross and to find there the meaning of our own life and death. What strikes me most in all that is read and said during these days is that Jesus of Nazareth did not die for himself, but for us, and that in following him we too are called to make our death a death for others. What makes you and me Christians is not only our belief that he who was without sin died for our sake on the cross and thus opened for us the way to his heavenly Father, but also that through his death our death is transformed from a totally absurd end of all that gives life its meaning into an event that liberates us and those whom we love. It is because of the liberating death of Christ that I dare say to you that mother's death is not simply an absurd end to a beautiful, altruistic life. Rather, her death is an event that allows her altruism to yield a rich harvest. Jesus died so that we might live, and everyone who dies in union with him participates in the life-giving power of his death. Thus we can indeed say that mother, who died under the sign of the cross, died so that we might live. Therefore, under that same sign, each of our deaths can become a death for others. I think that we need to start seeing the profound meaning of this dying for each other in and through the death of Christ in order to catch a glimpse of what eternal life might mean. Eternity is born in time, and every time someone dies whom we have loved dearly, eternity can break into our mortal existence a little bit more.

I am aware that I am barely touching the great mystery I want to give words to. But I think that the mystery is so deep and vast that we can enter it only slowly and with great care.

As we enter more deeply into the mysteries of this Holy Week and come closer to Easter, it will become clear what needs to be said. But now it seems of first importance to realize that when we begin seeing that mother died for us, we can also catch an insight into the meaning of our own death. Initially this insight might well be that the meaning of our death cannot be expressed in an idea, a concept, or a theory. Rather, it must be discovered as a truth less visible to us than to those for whom we die. This is perhaps why the meaning of mother's death is slowly revealing itself to us even though it remained hidden from her, and why the meaning of our death will remain more concealed from us than from those who will miss us most. To die for others implies that the meaning of our death is better understood by them than by ourselves. This requires of us great detachment and even greater faith. But most of all, it calls us to an ever increasing surrender to the ways in which God chooses to manifest his love to us.

6

*T*oday is Holy Thursday or, as you would say, White Thursday. As I continue this letter, I realize that this day enables me to write about death in a way that I could not before. As you know, Holy Thursday is the day of the Eucharist, the day on which Jesus took bread and wine and said to his intimate companions: "Take . . . eat . . . drink . . . this is my body . . . this is my blood . . . do this as a memorial of me." On the night before his death, Jesus gave us the gift of his lasting presence in our midst in order to remind us in the most personal way that his death was a death for us. That is why Paul remarks in his letter to the Corinthians, "Every time you eat this bread and drink this cup, you are proclaiming his death."

I am glad that I can write to you about mother's death and about our own death on this holy day because now I can see more clearly than ever how much the mystery of this day binds us together. My whole being is rooted in the Eucharist. For me, to be a priest means to be ordained to present Christ every day as food and drink to my fellow Christians. I sometimes wonder if those who are close to me are sufficiently aware of the fact that the Eucharist constitutes the core of my life. I do so many other things and have so many secondary identities—teacher, speaker, and writer—that it is easy to consider the Eucharist as the least important part of my life. But the opposite is true. The Eucharist is the center of my life and everything else receives its meaning from that center. I am saying this with so much emphasis in the hope that you will understand what I mean when I say that my life must be a continuing proclamation of the death and resurrection of Christ. It is first and foremost through the Eucharist that this proclamation takes place.

What has all of this to do with mother's death and with our death? A great deal, I think. Certainly much more than we might realize. You know better than I how important the Eucharist was for mother. There were few days in her adult life when she did not go to Mass and Communion. Although she did not speak much about it herself, we all knew that her daily participation in the Eucharist was at the center of her life. There were few things that remained so constant in her daily routine. Wherever she was or whatever she did, she always tried to find a nearby church to receive the gifts of Christ. Her great desire for this daily spiritual nourishment frequently led you to plan your trips in such a way that you both could attend Mass each day before resuming your travels.

I do not think I am exaggerating when I say that it was mother's deep and lasting devotion to the Eucharist that was one of the factors, if not the main factor, in my decision to become a priest. That is why this Holy Thursday is such an important day. It unites us in a very intimate way. The death of Christ as proclaimed in the Eucharist has given meaning to our lives in a way too deep for us to explain. What is important is the realization that through participation in the Eucharist, our lives and our deaths are being lifted up in the life and death of Christ. This is an enormously mysterious reality, but the more deeply we enter into it the more comfort and consolation we will find during these months of grief. Long before you, mother, or I was born, the death of Christ was celebrated in the Eucharist. And it will be celebrated long after we have died. During our few years of conscious participation in the Eucharist, our lives and deaths become part of this ongoing proclamation of the life and death of Christ. Therefore I dare to say that every time I celebrate the Eucharist and every time you receive the body and blood of Christ, we remember not only Christ's death but also her death, because it was precisely through the Eucharist that she was so intimately united with him.

This illuminates more fully that, in and through Christ, mother's death was a death for you and for me. By being united with Christ in the Eucharist, she participated in his life-giving death. Only Christ, the Son of God, could die not for himself but for others.

Mother's brokenness and sinfulness did not make it possible for her to die for others in complete self-surrender. But by eating the body and drinking the blood of Christ, her life was transformed into the life of Christ, and her death was lifted up into his death so that, living with Christ, she could also die with him. Thus, it is the death of Christ that gives meaning to her death. Hence we can say quite boldly that she died for us. Perhaps the sentence, "Christ died for us," has never before touched us in its full significance and has remained a rather abstract idea for both of us. But I think that mother's death can give us new insight into this central mystery of our faith. Once it starts making sense to us that mother died for our sake, and once we see that this was possible because of her intimate union with Christ through the Eucharist, we may also discover in a more personal way the ultimate meaning of Christ's death. Mother's death, then, directs our attention to the death of Christ and invites us to find in him the source of all our consolation and comfort.

I do not think that you would have said any of the things I have tried to say today. The language I have used does not come easily to you and the words are probably not the words you yourself would use. But on the other hand, I know that what I have written is not unfamiliar to you. Although you shared in mother's devotion to the Eucharist during her lifetime and joined her regularly in receiving the body and blood of Christ, during the last six months you have come to realize that you can experience a lasting bond with her through this great sacrament. It is my great hope that you will find an increasing strength from the Eucharist. Since you are living alone and often experience painful loneliness, the gifts of Christ, who died for you, can unite you in a very intimate way with him and so reveal to you the deeper meaning of mother's death. The Eucharist can never be fully explained or understood. It is a mystery to enter and experience from within. Every event of life can lead us to a deeper knowledge of the Eucharist. Marriage enables us to understand more deeply God's faithful love as it expresses itself in his lasting presence among us; illness and inner struggle can bring us more closely in touch with the healing power of the Eucharist; sin and personal failure can lead us to experience the Eucharist as a sacrament of forgiveness. What I am trying to say today is that mother's death can open our eyes to the Eucharist as a sacrament by which we proclaim Christ's death as a death for us, a death by which we are led to new life. Thus it can also help us to prepare for our own deaths. The more we see the Eucharist as a proclamation of Christ's death, the more we start seeing that our own deaths in communion with Christ cannot be in vain.

Thus the Eucharist brings us together in a very profound way. It is the core of my priesthood; it reveals the deeper meaning of mother's death; it helps us to prepare ourselves for our own deaths; and it points above all to Christ, who gives us his body and blood as a constant reminder that death is no longer a reason for despair but has become in and through him the basis of our hope. Therefore we will have the boldness to sing tomorrow in the liturgy, "We greet you cross, our only hope."

7

It might be that after all my words about the meaning of death you will get the impression that death is something to be desired; something that we can journey toward with expectation; something for which all of life prepares us; something, therefore, that is more or less the high point of life. If I have created such an impression, I need to correct it as soon as I can. Although I think it is possible to speak about the meaning of death, I also think that death is the one event against which we protest with all our being. We feel that life belongs to us and that death has no place in our basic desire to live. It is therefore not so surprising that most people, even older people, do not think much about death. As long as we feel healthy and vital, we prefer to keep our minds and bodies busy with the things of life. German theologian Karl Rahner calls death "the absurd arch-contradiction of existence," and indeed death does not make sense for anyone who can only make sense out of what he or she can understand in some way. But our total powerlessness in the face of death, in which any possibility of controlling our destiny is taken away from us, can hardly be perceived as having any value. Our whole being protests against the threat of non-being.

I am writing this on Good Friday. I have just participated in the liturgy, in which the death of Christ is remembered in the most moving way. I was asked to read the words Christ spoke during his passion. As I was pronouncing them in a loud voice so that all the monks and guests would be able to let them enter deeply into their hearts, I came to realize that Christ himself entered with us into the full experience of the absurdity of death. Jesus did not want to die. Jesus did not face his death as if he considered it a good to be striven for. He never spoke about death as something to be accepted gladly. Although he spoke about his death and tried to prepare his disciples for it, he never gave it morbid attention. And the Gospels contain no evidence that death was attractive to him. What we see in them is, rather, a deep inner protest against death. In the garden of Gethsemane, Jesus was gripped with fear and distress, and he prayed loudly to his Father: "Everything is possible for you. Take this cup away from me." This anguish became so intense that "his sweat fell to the ground like great drops of blood." And as he died on the Cross he cried out in agony: "My God, my God, why have you deserted me?"

Much more than the pain of his death, I think, it was death itself that filled Jesus with fear and agony.

For me this is a very important realization, because it undercuts any sentimentalizing or romanticizing of death. We do not want to die, even if we have to face—yes, befriend—our own death with all possible realism. Although we must befriend our death, that is, fully recognize it as a reality that is an intimate part of our humanity, death remains our enemy. Although we can and must prepare ourselves for death, we are never prepared for it. Although we have to see how death has been part of our life since birth, it remains the greatest unknown in our existence. Although we have to search for the meaning of death, our protest against it reveals that we will never be able to give it a meaning that can take our fear away.

Mother's death has made this very clear to us. You know how much her life was filled with the thought of God and his mysteries. Not only did she receive the Eucharist every day, but she spent many hours in prayer and meditation and read the holy Scriptures eagerly; she was also deeply grateful to everyone who supported her in her spiritual life. She had a very deep devotion to Mary, the Mother of God, and never went to sleep without asking for her prayers at the hour of her death. Indeed, mother's life was a life of preparation for death. But this did not make death easy for her. She never hesitated to say that she was afraid to die, that she did not feel prepared to appear before God, and that she was not yet ready to leave this world. She loved life, loved it to the full. She loved you with an unwavering devotion.

You are the person she always thought of and spoke about first; she would never allow anyone to distract her attention from you. Her children and grandchildren were her perennial concern and delight. Their joys were her joys, and their pains were her pains. And how she loved beauty: the beauty of nature with its flowers and trees, mountains and valleys; the beauty of the French cathedrals or old village churches; the beauty of the Italian cities, Ravenna, Florence, Assisi, and Rome. She could walk through these towns and cities and say with amazement, "Look, isn't it beautiful, look at that house, look at that church, look at those balconies with bougainvillea—isn't it lovely!" And she would be filled with joy and amazement. Yes, mother loved life. I still remember how she said to me, "Although I am old, I would like so much to live a few more years."

Death was hard and painful for her. In fact, I often think that it was precisely because her life of prayer had given her such a profound appreciation of all that is created, that it was so very hard for her to let it all go. The God she loved and for whom she wanted to give her life had shown her both the splendor of his creation and the complete finality with which death would cut her off from all she had learned to love.

As I reflect on mother's death, something that I could not see as clearly before is now becoming more visible to me. It is that death does not belong to God. God did not create death. God does not want death. God does not desire death for us. In God there is no death. God is a God of life. He is the God of the living and not of the dead. Therefore, people who live a deeply spiritual life, a life of real intimacy with God, must feel the pain of death in a particularly acute way. A life with God opens us to all that is alive. It makes us celebrate life; it enables us to see the beauty of all that is created; it makes us desire to always be where life is. Death, therefore, must be experienced by a really religious person neither as a release from the tension of life nor as an occasion for rest and peace, but as an absurd, ungodly, dark nothingness. Now I see why it is false to say that a religious person should find death easy and acceptable. Now I understand why it is wrong to think that a death without struggle and agony is a sign of great faith. These ideas do not make much sense once we realize that faith opens us to the full affirmation of life and gives us an intense desire to live more fully, more vibrantly, and more vigorously. If anyone should protest against death it is the religious person, the person who has increasingly come to know God as the God of the living.

This brings me back to the great mystery of today, the day we call Good Friday. It is the day on which Jesus, the Son of God, light of light, true God of true God, one in being with the Father, died. Indeed, on that Friday nearly two thousand years ago, outside the walls of Jerusalem, God died.

I hope you can feel with me that here lies the source of our consolation and hope. God himself, who is light, life, and truth, came to experience with us and for us the total absurdity of death. Jesus' death is not a memorable event because a good, holy prophet died. No, what makes the death of Jesus the main—and in a sense the only real—event in history is that the Son of God, in whom there was no trace of death, died the absurd death that is the fate of all human beings.

This gives us some idea of the agony of Jesus. Who has tasted life more fully than he? Who has known more intimately the beauty of the land in which he lived? Who has understood better the smiles of children, the cries of the sick, and the tears of those in grief? Every fiber of his being spoke of life. "I am the Way, the Truth and the Life," he said, and in him only life could be found. How will we ever be able to grasp what it must have meant for him to undergo death, to be cut off from life and to enter into the darkness of total destruction! The agony in the garden, the humiliation of the mockery, the pains of the flagellation, the sorrowful way to Calvary, and the horrendous execution on the Cross were suffered by the Lord of life.

I write this to you not to upset you but to console you in your grief. The Lord who died, died for us—for you, for me, for mother, and for all people. He died not because of any death or darkness in him, but only to free us from the death and darkness in us. If the God who revealed life to us, and whose only desire is to bring us to life, loved us so much that he wanted to experience with us the total absurdity of death, then—yes, then there must be hope; then there must be something more than death; then there must be a promise that is not fulfilled in our short existence in this world; then leaving behind the ones you love, the flowers and the trees, the mountains and the oceans, the beauty of art and music, and all the exuberant gifts of life cannot be just the destruction and cruel end of all things; then indeed we have to wait for the third day.

I am looking at the photograph you took of mother's grave. I look at the simple light brown wooden cross. The two heavy beams speak of strength. I read the words "In Peace," her name, "Maria," and the dates of her birth and death. They summarize it all. It is a lovely picture. What an exuberance of flowers! They really are splendid. With their white, yellow, red, and purple colors, they seem to lift up the cross and speak of life. Oh, how well I remember the 14th of October, six months ago today. What a beautiful morning that was! How gently the sun's rays covered the land when we carried her to this place! Do you remember? It was a sad day, but not only sad. There was a feeling of fulfillment, too. Her life had come to its fulfillment, and it had been such a gracious life. And there was gratitude in our hearts for her and for all who came to tell us what she had meant to them. It was a peaceful, quiet, and intimate day. I know you will never forget that day. Neither will I. It was the day that gave us strength to live on in quiet joy, not only looking backward but also forward.

Every time I look at that photograph of her grave, I experience again the new emotion that came to me after we buried her, an emotion so different from the emotion of seeing her again after a long absence, so different too from the emotion of watching her suffer and die. It is a new, very precious emotion. It is the emotion of a quiet, joyful waiting. Surely you know what I mean. There is a quiet contentment in this emotion. She has finished her life with us. She no longer has to suffer as we do; she no longer has to worry as we do; she no longer has to face the fear of death as we do. More than that, she will be spared the many anxieties and conflicts we still have to face. Nobody can harm her any more. We no longer have to protect her and be concerned about her health and safety. Oh, how we should love to have that concern again! But we have laid her to rest and she will not return. The rich soil in which we have buried her, the green hedges behind her grave, and the high lush trees around the small cemetery all create a feeling of safety, of being well received. But there is another side to this emotion. It includes waiting, quiet waiting. The solid, simple cross that stands above her grave speaks of something more than her death. Every time we go to that place, we sense that we are waiting, expecting, hoping. We wish to see her again and be with her once more, but we know that she has left us not to come back. At times, we wish to die and join her in death, but we know that we are called to live and to work on this earth. Our quiet, joyful waiting is much deeper than wishful thinking. It is waiting with the knowledge that love is stronger than death and that this truth will become visible to us. How? When? Where? These questions keep rushing into our impatient hearts. And yet, when we experience that quiet, joyful waiting, they cease troubling us and we feel that all is well.

You may have guessed, dear father, that I am writing this part to you on Holy Saturday. I have lived through this day many times, but this Saturday, April 14, 1979, is unique because today I have a new insight into what the quiet silence of this day means.

You know the story. They had laid him in the tomb that was in the garden close to the place where he was crucified. Joseph of Arimathea "rolled a stone against the entrance to the tomb" and "Mary of Magdala and Mary the mother of Joset were watching and took note of where he was laid." "Then they returned and prepared spices and ointments. And on the sabbath day they rested."

This is the quietest day of the year: no work, no great liturgical celebration, no visitors, no mail, no words. Just a very, very deep repose. A silent, in-between time. Lent is over but Easter has not yet come. He died, but we do not yet fully know what that means. The anxious, fearful tension of Good Friday is gone but no bells have yet been heard. A brother calls me to prayer with a wooden clapper. It has stopped raining. The raging storm that came over the valley last night has with-drawn, but clouds still cover the sky. Yes, a silent, joyful waiting. No panic, no despair, no screams, no tears or wringing of hands. No shouts of joy, either. No victori-ous songs, no banners or flags. Only a simple, quiet waiting with the deep, inner knowledge that all will be well. How? Do not ask. Why? Do not worry. Where? You will know. When? Just wait. Just wait quietly, peace-fully, joyfully . . . all will be well.

Sacred Saturday! The day on which we buried mother; the day on which we sit near Jesus' tomb and rest; the day on which monks look at each other as if they know something about which they are not yet allowed to speak. It is the day when I understand what your life has been like since you laid mother in her grave.

Do you feel what I am writing about? There are many, many questions, and we would like answers to them now. But it is too early. Nobody knows what to say. We saw that death is real. We saw that death took away from us the one we loved most. We stand by the grave. Let us not ask questions now. This is the time to let that inner quietude grow in us. The disciples thought that it was all over, finished, come to an end . . . if they thought much at all. The women wanted to take care of the grave. They prepared spices and ointments. But on Saturday, they all rested.

Doesn't this Holy Saturday give us a new insight into what our new life without mother can increasingly become? Doesn't this Holy Saturday tell us about this new emotion of quiet, joyful waiting in which we can grow steadily and securely? No longer do we have to cry; no longer do we have to feel the painful tearing away. Now we can wait, silencing all our wishes and fantasies about what will be, and simply hope in joy.

9

After I began to write this letter to you something happened that at first seemed rather insignificant to me. In the days following, however, it took on more and more importance. Therefore, I want to tell you about it before I finish this letter. It is a weather story. The weather here in upstate New York was lovely up until ten days ago. The winter was over, the spring had begun. The climate was mild and sunny, and the monks enjoyed walking through the woods and observing the first signs of the new season. Yellow, white, and blue crocuses decorated the yard, and everybody seemed happy that another cold season had come to an end. But not so! On the day I finally got myself organized enough to begin writing you this letter, a violent storm broke over the land, bringing with it heavy rains. Buckets appeared under the leaks in the roof, windows were shut securely, and no one ventured forth from the house. The temperature dropped sharply, and soon the rain turned into snow. The next day we were back in winter. It kept snowing the whole day, and I felt strangely disoriented. My whole body had been anticipating bright flowers, green trees, and songbirds, and this strange new weather felt totally incongruous. When the storm was over, the landscape seemed idyllic, like a Christmas card. The snow was fresh and beautiful and had settled on the green fields and fir trees like a fresh white robe. But I could not enjoy it. I simply kept saying to myself, "Well, one week from now it will be Easter and then it will be spring again." I discovered in myself a strange certainty that Easter would change the weather. And when everything was still pure white on Wednesday of Holy Week, I continued to feel, "Only three more days and everything will be green again!" Well, on Good Friday stormy winds rose up, a miserable rain began to come down, and it poured for the rest of the day. The next morning all the snow was gone. In the afternoon the clouds dissolved and a brilliant sun appeared, transforming everything into a joyous spectacle. When I looked out of my window and saw the fresh, clear light covering the meadows, I had a hard time not breaking the monastic silence! I walked out and went up to the ridge from which I could overlook the valley. I just smiled and smiled. And I spoke out loudly to the skies, "The Lord is risen; he is risen indeed!"

Never in my life have I sensed so deeply that the sacred events that we celebrate affect our natural surroundings. It was much more than the feeling of a happy coincidence. It was the intense realization that the events we were celebrating were the real events and that everything else, nature and culture included, was dependent on these events.

You will probably want to know now what the weather was like on Easter morning. It was gentle and cloudy. Nothing very unusual. No rain, no wind; not very cold, not very warm. No radiant sun, only a gentle, soft breeze. It did not really matter much to me. I would probably have been happy even if there had been snow again. What mattered to me was that I had come to experience during this holy season that the real events are the events that take place under the great veil of nature and history. All depends on whether we have eyes that see and ears that hear.

This is what I so much want to write to you on this Easter of 1979. Something very deep and mysterious, very holy and sacred, is taking place in our lives right where we are, and the more attentive we become the more we will begin to see and hear it. The more our spiritual sensitivities come to the surface of our daily lives, the more we will discover—uncover—a new presence in our lives. I have a strong sense that mother's death has been, and still is, a painful but very blessed purification that will enable us to hear a voice and see a face we had not seen or heard as clearly before.

Think of what is happening at Easter. A group of women go to the tomb, notice that the stone has been moved away, enter, see a young man in a white robe sitting on the righthand side, and hear him say, "He is not here." Peter and John come running to the tomb and find it empty. Mary of Magdala meets a gardener who calls her by name, and she realizes it is Jesus. The disciples, anxiously huddled together in a closed room, suddenly find him standing among them and hear him say, "Peace be with you." Two men come hurrying back from Emmaus and tell their puzzled friends that they met Jesus on the road and recognized him in the breaking of the bread. Later on, Simon Peter, Thomas, Nathanael, James, and John are fishing on the lake. A man on the shore calls to them, "Have you caught anything, friends?" They call back, "No." Then he says, "Throw the net out to starboard and you'll find something." They do, and when they catch so many fish that they cannot haul in their net, John says to Peter, "It is the Lord." And as these events are taking place, a new word is being spoken, at first softly and hesitatingly, then clearly and convincingly, and finally loudly and triumphantly, "The Lord is risen; he is risen indeed!"

I wonder how this story, the most important story of human history, speaks to you now that you know so well what it means to have lost the one you loved most. Have you noticed that none of the friends of Jesus, neither the women nor the disciples, had the faintest expectation of his return from death? His crucifixion had crushed all their hopes and expectations, and they felt totally lost and dejected. Even when Jesus appeared to them, they kept hesitating and doubting and needing to be convinced, not only Thomas but others as well. There was no trace of an "I-always-told-you-so" attitude. The event of Jesus' resurrection totally and absolutely surpassed their understanding. It went far beyond their own ways of thinking and feeling. It broke through the limits of their minds and hearts. And still, they believed—and their faith changed the world.

Isn't this good news? Doesn't this turn everything around and offer us a basis on which we can live with hope? Doesn't this put mother's death in a completely new perspective? It does not make her death less painful or our own grief less heavy. It does not make the loss of her less real, but it makes us see and feel that death is part of a much greater and much deeper event, the fullness of which we cannot comprehend, but of which we know that it is a life-bringing event. The friends of Jesus saw him and heard him only a few times after that Easter morning, but their lives were completely changed. What seemed to be the end proved to be the beginning; what seemed to be a cause for fear proved to be a cause for courage; what seemed to be defeat proved to be victory; and what seemed to be the basis for despair proved to be the basis for hope. Suddenly a wall becomes a gate, and although we are not able to say with much clarity or precision what lies beyond that gate, the tone of all that we do and say on our way to the gate changes drastically.

The best way I can express to you the meaning death receives in the light of the resurrection of Jesus is to say that the love that causes us so much grief and makes us feel so fully the absurdity of death is stronger than death itself. "Love is stronger than death." This sentence summarizes better than any other the meaning of the resurrection and therefore also the meaning of death. I have mentioned this earlier in this letter, but now you may better see its full meaning. Why has mother's death caused you so much suffering? Because you loved her so much. Why has your own death become such an urgent question for you? Because you love life, you love your children and your grandchildren, you love nature, you love art and music, you love horses, and you love all that is alive and beautiful. Death is absurd and cannot be meaningful for someone who loves so much.

The resurrection of Jesus Christ is the glorious manifestation of the victory of love over death. The same love that makes us mourn and protest against death will now free us to live in hope. Do you realize that Jesus appeared only to those who knew him, who had listened to his words and who had come to love him deeply? It was that love that gave them the eyes to see his face and the ears to hear his voice when he appeared to them on the third day after his death. Once they had seen and heard him and believed, the rest of their lives became a continuing recognition of his presence in their midst. This is what life in the Spirit of the risen Christ is all about. It makes us see that under the veil of all that is visible to our bodily eyes, the risen Lord shows us his inexhaustible love and calls us to enter even more fully into that love, a love that embraces both mother and us, who loved her so much.

It is with this divine love in our hearts, a love stronger than death, that our lives can be lived as a promise. Because this great love promises us that what we have already begun to see and hear with the eyes and ears of the Spirit of Christ can never be destroyed, but rather is "the beginning" of eternal life.

Today is the third day of Easter. Easter Tuesday. Here in the Trappist monastery it is the last day of the Easter festivities. For three days we have celebrated the resurrection of Jesus Christ, and it has been a real feast. Although the monks speak with each other only when necessary, and although there are no parties or parades, the Easter days have been more joyful than any I have celebrated in the past. The liturgies have been rich and exuberant with their many alleluias; the readings have been joyful and affirmative; the music has been festive; and everyone has been filled with gratitude toward God and each other.

On Easter Sunday I read the Gospel story about Peter and John running to the tomb and finding it empty. There were more than a hundred visitors in the abbey church, some from far away and some from nearby, some young and some old, some formally and some casually dressed. Sitting with forty monks around the huge rock that serves as the altar, they gave me a real sense of the Church. After reading the Gospel, I preached. I had seldom preached on Easter Sunday during my twenty-two years of priesthood, and I felt very grateful that I could announce to all who were present: "The Lord is risen; he is risen indeed." Everyone listened with great attention and I had a sense that the risen Christ was really among us, bringing us his peace. During the Eucharist, I prayed for you, for mother, and for all who are dear to us. I felt that the risen Christ brought us all together, bridging not only the distance between Holland and the United States but also that between life and death. Lent was long, some-times very hard, and not without its dark moments and tempting demons. But now, in the light of the resurrec-tion of Christ, Lent seems to have been short and easy. I guess this is true for all of life. In darkness we doubt that there will ever be light, but in the light we soon forget how much darkness there was.

Now there is light. In fact, the sun has even broken through and the large stretches of blue sky now visible behind the clusters of clouds remind me again that often what we see is not what is most enduring.

Dear father, this seems the most natural time to con-clude not only the Easter celebration but also this letter. For twelve days I have been reflecting on mother's death in the hope of offering you and myself some comfort and consolation. I do not know if I have been able to reach you in your loneliness and grief. Maybe my words often said more to me than to you. But even if this is so, I still hope that the simple fact that these words have been written by your son about her whom we have both loved so much will be a source of consolation to you.